NORTH SARASOTA PUBLIC LIBRARY

2801 NEWTOWN BLVD.
SARASOTA, FL 34234

31969024298662

NANOTECHNOLOGY

▲ by Janet Slingerland

NORTH SARASOTA
PUBLIC LIBRARY
2801 NEWTOWN BLVD.
SARASOTA, FL 34234

Content Consultant

L. Jay Guo
Professor of Electrical
Engineering and Computer Science
University of Michigan

Essential Library

An Imprint of Abdo Publishing | abdopublishing.com

CUTTING EDGE
SCIENCE +
TECHNOLOGY

abdopublishing.com

Published by Abdo Publishing, a division of ABDO, PO Box 398166, Minneapolis, Minnesota 55439. Copyright © 2016 by Abdo Consulting Group, Inc. International copyrights reserved in all countries. No part of this book may be reproduced in any form without written permission from the publisher. Essential Library™ is a trademark and logo of Abdo Publishing.

Printed in the United States of America, North Mankato, Minnesota
092015
012016

THIS BOOK CONTAINS
RECYCLED MATERIALS

Cover Photo: Shutterstock Images
Interior Photos: Bernd Thissen/Picture-Alliance/DPA/AP Images, 4–5; Rex Features/AP Images, 8; Volodymyr Krasyuk/Shutterstock Images, 10; Everett Collection/Newscom, 11; Ivan Garcia/Shutterstock Images, 13; Joanna Wnuk/iStockphoto, 14 (right); iStockphoto, 14 (left), 26–27, 36–37, 47 (top right), 47 (bottom left), 47 (top middle), 47 (bottom right); Zhukov/Shutterstock Images, 15 (left); Matthias G. Ziegler/Shutterstock Images, 15 (right); Edelmann/AP Images, 16–17; Peter Hermes Furian/iStockphoto, 19; Christopher Futcher/iStockphoto, 20; Dartmouth College Electron Microscope Facility, 23; Steve Gschmeissner/Science Photo Library/Getty Images, 24; Red Line Editorial, 29; Stephanie Zollshan/The Berkshire Eagle/AP Images, 31; Jordan Kartholl/Journal & Courier/AP Images, 34; He Huan/Imaginechina/AP Images, 41; Shan He/Imaginechina/AP Images, 43; Jon Super/AP Images, 45; Shutterstock Images, 46, 47 (top left), 65; Martin Vloet/University of Michigan, 48–49; Paul Sakuma/AP Images, 51, 59; George Widman/AP Images, 53; Per Lindgren/REX/Newscom, 55; CB2/ZOB/WENN.com/Newscom, 62–63; Adrian Li/Rex Features/AP Images, 69; ZJAN/Surrey NanoSystems/Newscom, 71; Mark Blinch/The Canadian Press/AP Images, 72–73; Jeff Fitlow/Rice University, 76; Mindaugas Kulbis/AP Images, 79; Yuriy Rudyy/Shutterstock Images, 80–81; Rice University, 83; Robyn Beck/AFP/Getty Images, 85; Jens Wolf/Picture-Alliance/DPA/AP Images, 87; Larissa Lee Beck/Picture-Alliance/DPA/AP Images, 88–89; Michael Reichel/Picture-Alliance/DPA/AP Images, 91; Amelie Benoist/BSIP/BSIP/Corbis, 93; Guido Vrola/iStockphoto, 94; Eric Heller/Science Source, 97; Bill Hogan/MCT/Newscom, 99

Editor: Nick Rebman
Series Designer: Craig Hinton

Library of Congress Control Number: 2015910689

Cataloging-in-Publication Data
Slingerland, Janet.
 Nanotechnology / Janet Slingerland.
  p. cm. -- (Cutting-edge science and technology)
 ISBN 978-1-62403-917-1 (lib. bdg.)
 Includes bibliographical references and index.
 1. Nanotechnology--Juvenile literature.   I. Title.
 620.5--dc23

CONTENTS

ONE

TINY TECHNOLOGY

Swimming was the sport to watch at the 2008 Beijing Olympics. A total of 25 world records were broken. The only Olympics where more swimming records were broken occurred in 1976, the year contestants could wear goggles for the first time.[1] Of the records set in Beijing, all but one of the swimmers wore Speedo's latest swimsuit. The suit seemed to be a record-generating machine, winning three world records in its first week. In the six months between the suit's debut and the Olympics, swimmers wearing it broke a total of 48 records.[2]

The LZR Racer, a full-body swimsuit, was the culmination of three years of development that included help from NASA scientists. A key ingredient in the success of the suit was its fabric, which was designed to reduce drag from the water as much as possible while maximizing support of the swimmers' muscles. The fabric was a "very high-density weave," which compressed the swimmers' bodies to streamline

Most swimmers in the 2008 Summer Olympics wore LZR Racer suits, which used nanotechnology to make the suits faster.

them. The fabric then went through a nanotechnology treatment that changed the molecular structure of the surface of the material. The process resulted in fabric that absorbed only 2 percent of its weight in water, compared with the 50 percent absorbed by the previous competitive swimsuit fabric.[3]

The governing board for international swimming competition, Fédération Internationale de Natation (FINA), banned the LZR Racer and similar suits in 2010. This ban addressed accusations that competitors with expensive, state-of-the-art swimsuits had an unfair technological advantage. FINA dictated that suits had to be "thicker than one millimeter; made of material with limited buoyancy; and expose the neck, shoulders and ankles of the athlete."[4]

Despite FINA's modified swimsuit requirements, companies still use technology to improve their products. Many use nanotechnology-based finishes that add to or modify less than 100 nanometers of the fabric's surface to repel water. These finishes typically trap air bubbles on the surface, preventing water from reaching the material's fibers. As nanotechnology increasingly plays a role in sports equipment, the debate continues as to how much technology in sports is too much.

▲Nano Sports

Many sports have already embraced nanotechnology. Carbon nanotubes are added to bike frames, tennis rackets, baseball bats, hockey sticks, and golf clubs to strengthen them while keeping them light. Tennis balls with clay nanoparticles retain their air, keeping them bouncier longer. Ice-skating blades stay super sharp thanks to ceramic nanoparticles. Nanocoatings on exercise clothing help it block the sun's ultraviolet rays, stay drier, and resist odors.

The Science of Small

Nanotechnology is a confusing discipline. Is it science? Is it engineering? Is it natural or man-made? The answer to all these questions is yes. The National Nanotechnology Initiative describes nanotechnology as "science, engineering, and technology conducted at the nanoscale, which is about 1 to 100 nanometers."[5]

A meter is a little taller than the height of an average countertop. That meter is made up of a billion nanometers. As a comparison, imagine Earth represents a meter. A nanometer would then be the equivalent of a marble. A man-made transistor, found in an integrated circuit inside a computer or cell phone, measures less than 30 nanometers in size. A virus cell varies from 60 to 200 nanometers.[6]

Nanotechnology deals with transistors, viruses, and more. It covers a broad spectrum of disciplines including chemistry, biology, materials science, physics, and engineering. Dr. K. Eric Drexler, one of the pioneers of nanotechnology, once lamented, "I know of no other field . . . defined by a criterion as generic as size."[7]

Historical Nanoparticles

Humans have been using nanoparticles in man-made objects for thousands of years. Long ago, artisans did not realize they were working with nanotechnology; their remarkable works were the result of trial and error.

An ancient Roman artisan created an extraordinary piece of work now known as the Lycurgus Cup. The images surrounding the cup are splendid, but what is really special about this cup is its color. Initially, the cup appears opaque green. Shine a light through it, however, and the cup glows translucent red. Scientists now know nanosized gold and silver particles suspended in the glass create this magical effect. Similar techniques were used to create the rich colors for medieval stained-glass windows.

The Lycurgus Cup appears to change color depending on how it is lit.

In the 1600s, sword maker Assad Ullah produced exceptionally flexible, strong, and sharp weapons known as Damascus sabers. Ullah's exact technique is unknown, but modern science has proved it featured carbon nanotubes and other nanostructures incorporated into the steel. The nanostructures are what gave Damascus sabers their incredible powers.

Atomically Speaking

In 1959, IBM was producing state-of-the-art computers that took up the space of a small room. So it was rather surprising when physicist Richard P. Feynman decided to think small.

In December of that year, Feynman gave a speech to the American Physical Society titled "Plenty of Room at the Bottom." In the speech, Feynman challenged scientists to think about "manipulating and controlling things on a small scale."[8] Feynman was not thinking miniature; he was thinking on the scale of atoms and nanometers.

Feynman spoke of storing all 24 volumes of the Encyclopaedia Britannica, approximately 24,000 pages, on the head of a pin. He predicted a future in which computers with millions of transistors could perform complex functions such as recognizing people's faces. He mused, "What would the properties of materials be if we could really arrange the atoms the way we want them?"[9] Although he did not use the term *nanotechnology*, the advances Feynman dreamed of all fall under the field as it is now known.

It took decades for Feynman's ideas to catch on. In the meantime, the scientific world focused on conquering space. Computers were integral to the space program and were used increasingly in business. Both areas demanded smaller, faster, and more complex computers, spurring the march toward the nanoscale.

Integrated circuits, or microchips, have been getting smaller over time.

It was not until the 1980s that nanotechnology really started to spread. The invention of several microscopes in that decade finally allowed scientists to view nanoscale items.

Nano Now

According to the Project on Emerging Nanotechnologies, there are more than 1,600 consumer products containing nanomaterials.[10] Nanoparticles are used as additives in a wide variety of products, including motor oil and deodorant. Electronics such as cell phones and computers contain millions or even billions of nanoscale components in the form of transistors. Nanoscale treatments keep surfaces scratch- or dirt-free. Odor-free and waterproof fabrics often get their properties from nanotechnology. And nanotechnology is improving the quality and efficiency of many television and electronic displays.

Richard **Feynman**

(1918–1988)

Richard Feynman grew up in New York City. He had his own home laboratory by age ten thanks to his father's hope that he would be a scientist. By age 15, he had taught himself trigonometry, algebra, analytic geometry, and calculus.

Feynman earned a bachelor's degree in physics from the Massachusetts Institute of Technology (MIT) in 1939 and a PhD from Princeton University in 1942. During World War II (1939–1945), he worked on the Manhattan Project, which led to the development of the atomic bomb.

After the war, Feynman became a professor of theoretical physics. He received the 1965 Nobel Prize in Physics for his work with quantum electrodynamics (QED) and the creation of Feynman diagrams. QED addresses the electromagnetic forces between charged particles such as electrons and positrons. Feynman diagrams are a graphical representation of these interactions.

In 1986, Feynman helped determine why the Space Shuttle *Challenger* exploded. He concluded the report with one of his famous sayings: "For a successful technology, reality must take precedence over public relations, for nature cannot be fooled."[11]

Large-scale nanomanufacturing processes that produce quality nanomaterials are still being researched and developed. These processes fall into two categories. Top-down approaches start with full-sized materials and break them down into nano sizes. The making of computer components falls in this category. By contrast, bottom-up approaches build materials at an atomic or molecular level, often employing complicated chemical processes to result in the desired materials.

Many more applications of nanotechnology are being studied in universities and research and development departments around the world. But before they could make these advances, scientists had to be able to see the nanomaterials they were working with.

New smartphones typically have more than one billion transistors.

NANOMETER
PERSPECTIVES

I t can be difficult to grasp just how small a nanometer (nm) is. Here are some examples to help put the nanometer in perspective:

» A grain of table sugar averages 500,000 nm in size.

» A piece of paper is 100,000 to 200,000 nm thick.

» A human hair is between 60,000 and 100,000 nm in diameter.

» A grain of powdered sugar averages 11,000 nm in size.

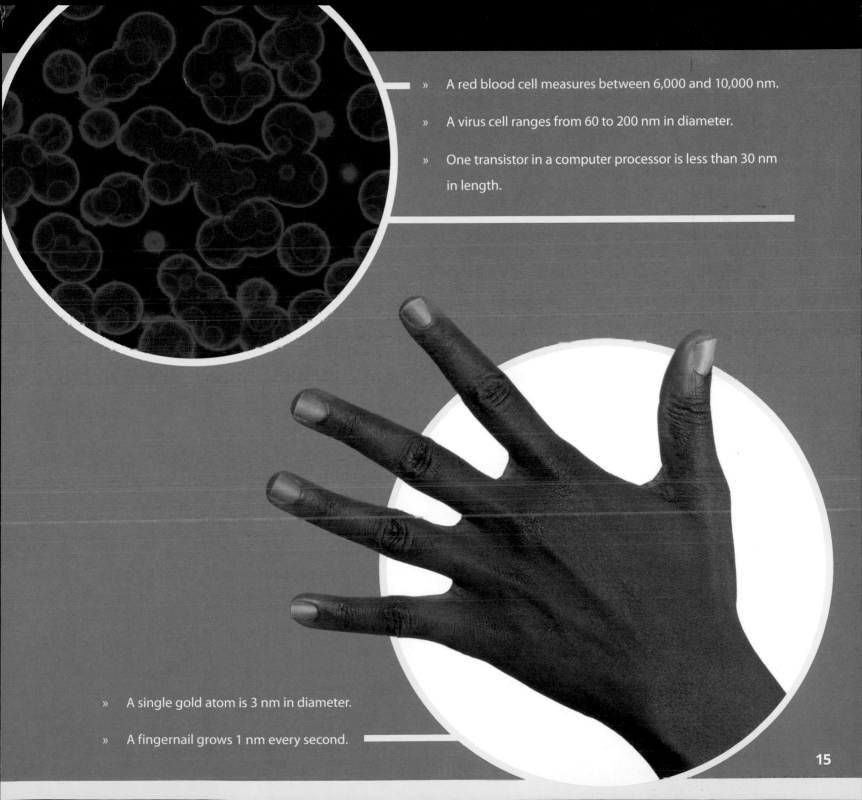

» A red blood cell measures between 6,000 and 10,000 nm.

» A virus cell ranges from 60 to 200 nm in diameter.

» One transistor in a computer processor is less than 30 nm in length.

» A single gold atom is 3 nm in diameter.

» A fingernail grows 1 nm every second.

TWO

VIEWING THE
NANOVERSE

German scientist and engineer Gerd Binnig described the first time he was able to view a sample of gold at the atomic level: "I could not stop looking at the images. It was like entering a new world."[1]

Most humans can see nothing smaller than 100 microns (100,000 nm), about the width of a human hair.[2] The technology that allowed Binnig and his research partner, Heinrich Rohrer, to see something 100,000 times smaller built on the work of many scientists over thousands of years. The difficulty in viewing something so small stems from the limitations of the human eye. Humans can see only visible light, a very small portion of the light available in the electromagnetic spectrum.

Heinrich Rohrer, left, and Gerd Binnig, right, developed a microscope that enabled them to see things at an atomic level.

Waves of Light

When most people think of waves, they think of water rising and falling on an ocean or lake. Others may think of sound waves. Both water and sound waves are types of mechanical waves—that is, waves formed by disturbances or vibrations in a medium. Beach waves are vibrations in water, while sound waves are vibrations in air. Mechanical waves need a medium such as water or air in which to travel, and they move by transferring energy from one particle in the medium to the next. Sound cannot travel in a vacuum; a vacuum contains no particles to which energy can be transferred.

There is another type of wave people interact with on a constant basis: electromagnetic waves. Electromagnetic waves are formed by vibrations of electric and magnetic fields. Unlike mechanical waves, electromagnetic waves do not need to travel through a medium. They can travel through air and solids, but they can also travel through a vacuum. These waves travel at the speed of light. They are, in fact, forms of light waves.

The electromagnetic spectrum describes the range of possible electromagnetic waves. Waves can be described by their frequency, their wavelength, or their energy. Frequency defines the number of waves that occur within a one-second time span. If waves occur once per second, they have a frequency of 1 hertz (Hz); if they occur twice per second, they have a frequency of 2 Hz. The wavelength is the distance from a point in one wave to the same point in the next wave.

As the wavelength shortens, a wave's frequency and energy increase. Waves with longer wavelengths have lower frequencies and less energy. The X rays used to image bones inside bodies at the doctor's office fall at the short-wavelength, high-energy side of the spectrum. Radio waves have longer wavelengths, lower frequencies, and lower energy. The visible light that people see falls in a very

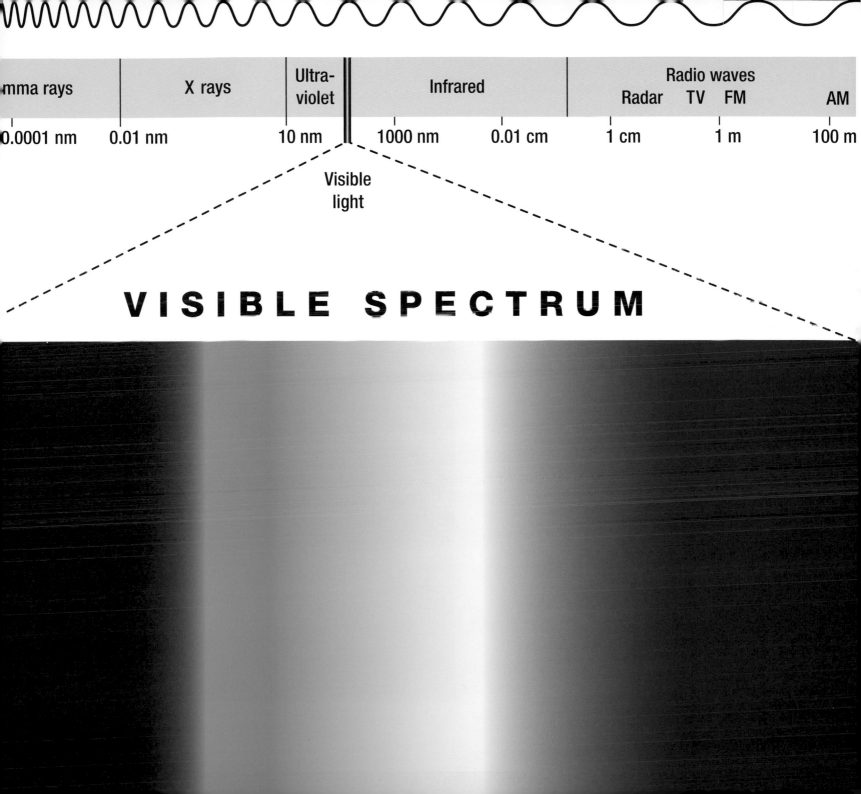

The resolution of compound light microscopes is limited by the range of visible light.

small range of wavelengths between 400 and 700 nanometers.[3]

Optical Viewing

The first microscopes appeared in the 1600s. These single-lens optical microscopes were not much different from a magnifying glass, a single lens that bends light so a viewer can see a larger version of the specimen. Over time, improvements utilized multiple and more complex lenses to provide better quality images at higher magnification. It is important for a microscope not only to enlarge the image but to provide adequate resolution as well. Resolution is the ability to distinguish between closely spaced objects and to see sharp rather than blurry edges.

The microscope most widely known and commonly used in schools is an optical microscope called the compound light microscope. Thin samples of a specimen are mounted on a glass

Microsphere Magic

While electron microscopes provide remarkable views of the nanoworld, they have many limitations. The microscopes are expensive and require extensive training to use. The preparation of the samples prior to viewing is critical and often requires the use of toxic materials. The samples are held in a vacuum during scanning; therefore, if a live sample was not killed by the toxic chemicals during preparation, it would certainly die during scanning. Images provided by electron microscopes might not be entirely accurate, either. Any colorization on the image is artificial, and the interaction of the electrons with the sample during scanning may alter the sample.

Scientists may have found a way to improve optical microscopes so they can see living organisms at the nanoscale. Researchers at the University of Manchester in the United Kingdom discovered in 2011 that placing glass microspheres, tiny glass balls, on top of a sample under an optical microscope improved its resolution. Using microspheres with diameters between 2,000 and 9,000 nanometers, Dr. Lin Li was able to see down to 50 nanometers.[5] Skeptics pointed out the team viewed only stationary, inorganic objects.

Still, Dr. Li was excited about his discovery. "The surprising thing is the simplicity," he said. "One hundred dollars buys you about 100 million microspheres. Using conventional optical microscopes, almost anyone can do this."[6]

Initially, other researchers had difficulty replicating the process. But by the end of 2013, Swiss researchers had used the method to view biological objects including mitochondria and chromosomes in cells.

slide A light source provides the illumination from below, passing through several lenses and the specimen to provide the viewer with a magnified image. Even the best compound microscope cannot resolve details that are closer than 200 nanometers.[4]

Seeing with Electrons

In 1933, German engineer Ernst Ruska built the first transmission electron microscope (TEM). This microscope works much like a light microscope, but instead of shining light through a sample, it transmits an electron beam through it. Instead of using glass to control beams of light, magnets control

NanoArt

The unique view of the universe provided by state-of-the-art microscopes has inspired a new generation of art. NanoArt merges art and science at the nanoscale. In some cases, artists manipulate atoms and molecules into nanosculptures. Some artists add artistic layers to images captured from the various nanoscale microscopic techniques. Yet others replicate nanoscale structures on a grand scale.

In 2014, Cornell University turned its campus into a showcase for NanoArt. One of the key pieces in the show was a 46-foot- (14 m) tall sculpture called *A Needle Woman*, which people could enter one at a time to view from the inside. The colors seen in the transparent panels changed with the light, creating the iridescent effect seen on many beetles and butterflies. These panels were made from a nano polymer, a material engineered at the molecular level to refract incoming light into many different wavelengths.

That same year also saw the third International Festival of NanoArt. Materials scientist Chris Orfescu curated the festival, which included art of his own. Orfescu's art starts with nanolandscapes or nanosculptures created by chemical or physical processes. After capturing these elements using a scanning electron microscope, he digitally manipulates and colors the image, creating the final piece of art.

a beam of electrons. If the electrons hit a dense portion in the sample, they scatter. Electrons pass through the other areas unhindered. After the beam passes through the sample, the electrons collect on a viewing screen, creating a shadow image of the sample. One of the drawbacks of the TEM is that the sample must be extremely thin—less than 100 nanometers thick.[7]

The TEM as originally designed creates two-dimensional, black-and-white images of the sample. The use of computer software and multiple TEM images of the same sample taken from different angles have allowed scientists to create three-dimensional images.

In the 1950s, a new version of the electron microscope evolved. The scanning electron microscope (SEM) uses the same principles as the TEM. Instead of shining the electron beam through the sample,

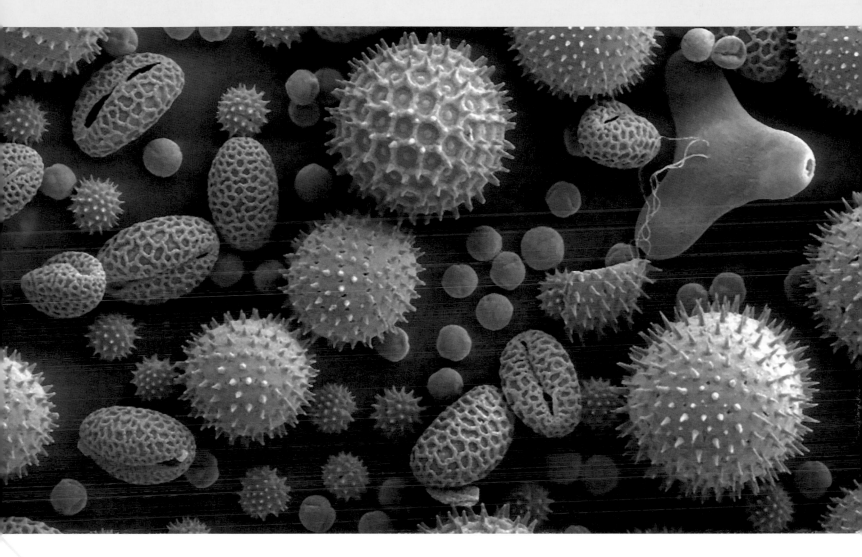

Scientists took a photograph of pollen using a scanning electron microscope. The smallest grains are approximately 6,000 nanometers in diameter.

however, the SEM bounces the electrons off the sample. SEM images are created from electrons reflected off the sample along with electrons generated by the sample. These images are black and white, but they provide a three-dimensional surface view of the sample.

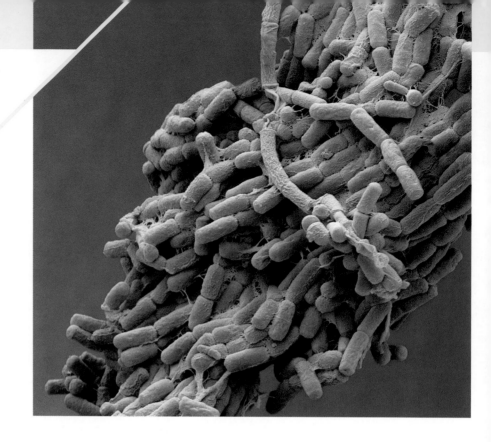

A scanning electron microscope revealed details of E. coli bacteria.

Modern electron microscopes can magnify objects up to 2 million times, but they still use the same basic technology Ruska used. The incredibly detailed images provided by these microscopes come at a cost. The devices are expensive to buy and maintain, and they require a significant amount of reliable electricity to operate. Successful use of electron microscopes requires extensive training, making it a highly specialized skill.

Probing Views

IBM researchers Gerd Binnig and Heinrich Rohrer were not satisfied with the resolution provided by electron microscopes. They wanted to view things at an atomic level. In 1981, Binnig and Rohrer created the scanning tunneling microscope (STM), the first in a series of scanning probing microscopes.

A probe with a very sharp tip, as thin as a single atom, is held about an atom's length away from the sample. The probe scans the sample in a motion called a raster pattern, repeatedly moving across the width of the sample, moving down a line, and then back across the sample. The probe follows the contour of the sample, feeling where it rises and dips. The probe also measures the electric current caused by electrons moving or tunneling from the sample to the probe, providing information about the atomic details on the surface of the sample. In order for tunneling to take place, both the tip and the sample must be conductors or semiconductors, or materials in which electricity is able to flow.

In 1986, Binnig extended the STM to create the atomic force microscope (AFM), another type of scanning probe microscope that could image nonconductive materials, or materials in which electricity could not flow. Rather than measuring electric current as the STM does, the AFM measured the forces between the atoms, known by scientists as van der Waals forces. Since scanning probe microscopes first appeared, scientists have modified them to study various aspects of samples as well as to manipulate samples at the atomic level. Thanks to these improvements, scanning microscopes remain the best tools scientists have for viewing super-small materials.

◢ Nobel Worthy

The transmission electron microscope and scanning tunneling microscope revolutionized the way scientists viewed the world. In 1986, Ernst Ruska, Gerd Bennig, and Heinrich Rohrer shared the Nobel Prize in Physics in recognition of these inventions. The Nobel committee declared the TEM "one of the most important inventions of this century." They also credited the STM with opening up "entirely new fields . . . for the study of the structure of matter."[8]

THREE

NANOPARTICLES

Particles at the nanoscale do not behave as they do at the macro or normal scale. Aluminum demonstrates this behavior in spectacular fashion. On the macro scale, it is an inert metal, used widely in soda cans and food wraps. But when aluminum is ground down to 30-nanometer particles, it explodes in air—making it a perfect catalyst for rocket fuel.[1]

The surprising behavior of nanoparticles stems from two things. Larger-sized materials follow the classical rules of physics, such as Newton's laws of motion. When materials become nanosized, however, they become subject to the rules of quantum physics, which can make objects behave very differently. Nanoparticles are also more reactive than larger versions of the same material due to their increased surface area. These factors allow previously opaque materials such as zinc oxide to become transparent, and stable items such as aluminum to become combustible.

When quantum physics takes over, objects do not react in expected ways. Imagine throwing a ball at a wall. Classical physics states that the ball will always bounce off the wall; but the laws of quantum physics say the ball will sometimes pass

Aluminum, similar to many materials, behaves differently depending on the size of its particles.

through the wall. This is the theory of quantum tunneling, which is the basis for the scanning tunneling microscope and computer transistors. This ability is related to the quantum rule called wave-particle duality, which states that particles can act as waves and waves can act as particles.

In classical physics, a material has the same properties regardless of its size. A boulder has the same properties as a grain of sand if they are made from the same material. At the nanoscale, when the rules of quantum physics take effect, the properties of the material change as the size of the material changes. Scientists view these properties as tunable; they are able to manipulate the material to have the properties they want by changing the size of the nanoparticles. Tunable properties include melting point, the ability to carry electricity, and color.

The size of nanoparticles not only gives them quantum properties; it also makes them more reactive than larger scale materials due to their increased surface area per volume of material. To illustrate, imagine a solid cube. It has six sides exposed to the air. If each side measures one centimeter, each side has an area of one square centimeter, and the cube has a total surface area of six square centimeters. Now imagine a bunch of one-millimeter cubes stacked up like building blocks to make a one-centimeter cube. It would take 1,000 of the one-millimeter cubes to fill up the same space as a one-centimeter cube. Each one-millimeter cube has a surface area of six square millimeters, which is equal to 0.06 square centimeters. The total surface area for the 1,000 one-millimeter cubes is 60 square centimeters.

Now imagine the space within a one-centimeter cube filled with one-nanometer cubes. It would take a sextillion cubes to fill the space; a sextillion is a 1 followed by 21 zeroes. Each nanometer cube has a surface area of six square nanometers, resulting in a total surface area of 60 sextillion square nanometers, or 60 million square centimeters—an area larger than a football field.

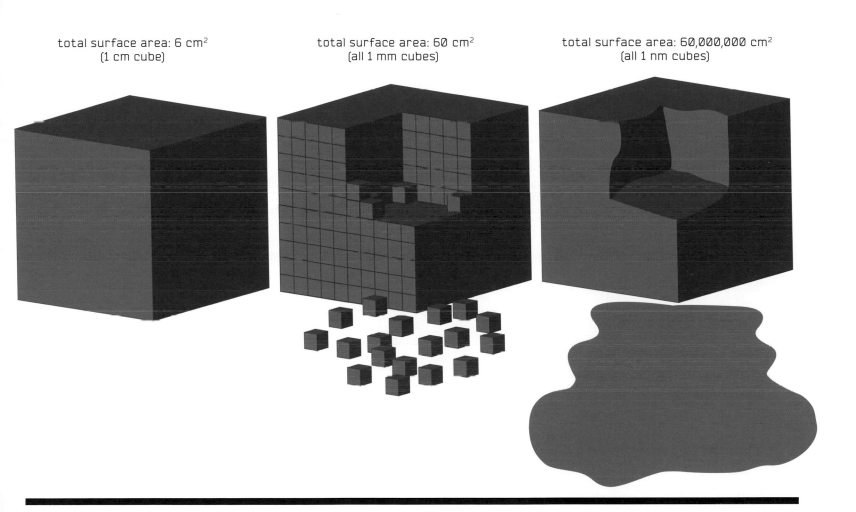

total surface area: 6 cm²
(1 cm cube)

total surface area: 60 cm²
(all 1 mm cubes)

total surface area: 60,000,000 cm²
(all 1 nm cubes)

Tubes, Wires, and Flakes

Nanomaterials are typically named based on the shape and dimension of their particles. Common names are tubes, wires, films, flakes, and shells. Some are referred to simply as nanoparticles. In order to classify as nano, one or more of the dimensions of each particle must be on the nanoscale, between one and 100 nanometers.

Nanoparticles typically have all dimensions on the nanoscale. Nanotubes have a nanoscale diameter, but they can be millimeters long or more. Nanofilms and nanoplates have nanoscale thicknesses, but their length and width can be much larger.

Additional surface area gives the material more chances to react to other substances it contacts. This concept is illustrated in the Mentos geyser experiment: dropping a pack of Mentos candy into a bottle of soda causes the soda to shoot into the air. Students at Appalachian State University viewed Mentos using a scanning electron microscope. They saw that the candies were covered with micron-scale bumps and ridges, resulting in a dramatic increase in surface area. As the Mentos fall through the soda, the candies provide surfaces that react with the carbon dioxide in the soda, allowing for the growth of gas bubbles.

The Mentos soda geyser is possible because of the candies' large surface area.

Getting a Lift

The special properties of nanoparticles make them suitable for a wide range of applications. By moving to nanoparticles for fingerprinting, scientists found they worked in situations where conventional materials did not. The use of fingerprints as identification goes as far back as ancient China. Aside from DNA, fingerprints are the only characteristic that is unique and identifiable for each individual. Since the early 1900s, they have been a staple in criminal trials.

When people touch objects, they leave behind fingerprints, most of which are invisible to the human eye. These latent or hidden fingerprints are composed of deposits excreted from sweat glands

in the skin. Crime scene investigators use special powders that stick to these deposits, illuminating the fingerprint. Ideally, this powder sticks to only the ridges and swirls that make up the fingerprint. Only a fingerprint with proper clarity can be matched conclusively.

Traditional techniques use materials such as carbon black and aluminum flake, which adhere to the sweat residue in the latent print. This works approximately half the time on surfaces such as paper, and it does not work at all in wet conditions. Particles in these powders measure between one and ten micrometers, up to a thousand times larger than nanoscale materials.

Researchers at Sydney University in Australia reported in 2007 that 20-nanometer zinc oxide powders provide clearer prints. These powders also glow under ultraviolet (UV) light and work in wet conditions. Nanoparticles can also help retrieve latent prints from paper surfaces. Gold nanoparticles dusted on the surface adhere to any part of the paper where the fingers have not touched, but they do not stick to places where the finger touched. When a solution containing silver nanoparticles is applied, the gold particles turn black, leaving a negative image of the fingerprint.

Fingerprints and Nanotechnology

A person's fingerprint determines more than his or her identity. In 2007, researchers at the University of East Anglia in the United Kingdom discovered the sweat deposits in fingerprints contain significant amounts of information. This includes traces of metabolites, chemicals produced when a body is processing food, drink, or drugs it has ingested or inhaled.

That same year, the company Intelligent Fingerprinting spun off to produce a handheld device that would determine whether a person had been using drugs or alcohol by processing his or her fingerprint. The device, set to be commercially available in 2015, could be used to ensure a worker is

Nanoprotection

Many people use nanoparticles every day without even knowing it. Most modern sunscreens contain 25- to 50-nanometer-sized particles of zinc oxide and titanium dioxide, materials proven to be great barriers against the sun's damaging UV rays.[2] Years ago, lifeguards were famous for having a thick white paste covering their noses. They were using the same materials, but on a larger scale. The larger particle sizes reflected visible light, making the skin look white. The use of nanoparticles in sunscreen eliminates the white-faced look. Although the particles maintain their UV-blocking abilities, their nano size allows them to absorb and scatter light, providing for transparent sun protection. In addition to being clearer and feeling lighter on the skin, the nanosized versions of these sun blockers last longer, requiring less frequent applications.

Many people have expressed concern about rubbing nanoparticles on their bodies. A study in 2010 found less than 0.01 percent of the zinc nanoparticles in sunscreen were able to penetrate the skin.[3]

In 2014, Australian researcher Simon James reported that even if some of the zinc oxide nanoparticles made their way through the skin, the human body could handle it. A specific white blood cell called a macrophage eliminates the particles before they reach the bloodstream. James said, "In the case of these nanoparticles, there was no real sign of overt toxicity in sunscreens or in other consumer products."[4]

fit for duty in a safety-critical job such as flying a plane. Other potential uses include workplace drug screening and roadside driver checks.

To perform traditional tests, blood, urine, or saliva is required. However, these bodily fluids have the potential to expose the person gathering the sample to deadly diseases. There is also a chance for the sample to be switched or contaminated. The Intelligent Fingerprinting device captures a fingerprint and does all testing, eliminating these risks and tying the test results to the fingerprint.

The device contains antibody-coated nanoparticles. Each antibody is a protein that links only to one specific metabolite. The device displays when an antibody-metabolite match has been found,

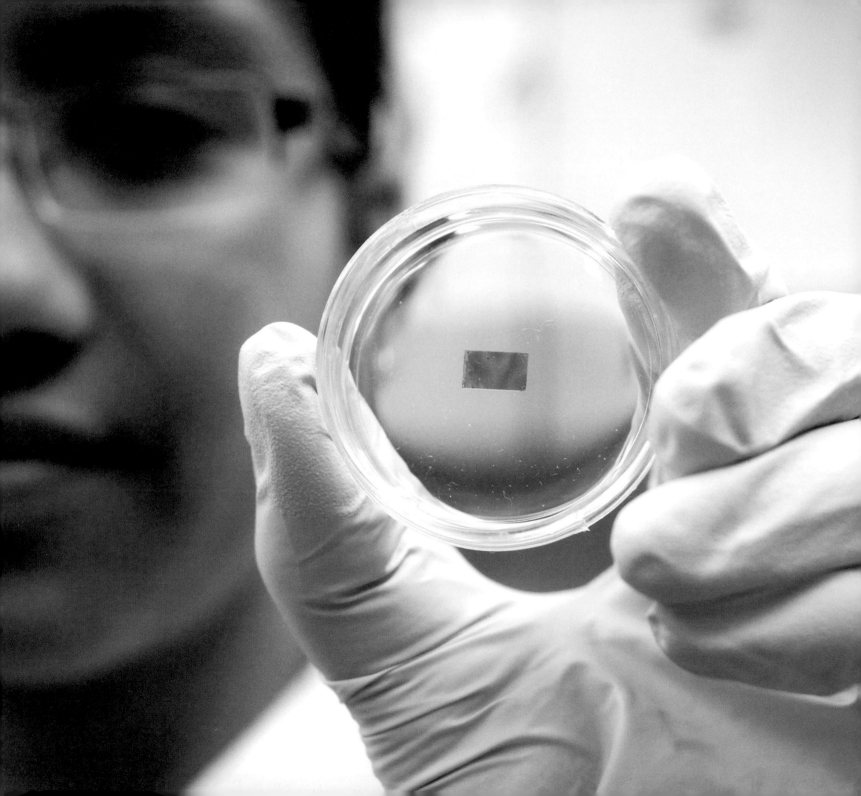

A researcher shows a microchip that can detect tiny chemical changes.

indicating the person recently used the substance being tested for. Because the device tests for signs the body has been processing a drug or alcohol, it will not show a false positive if the person came in contact with the substance without using it.

CARBON CRAZE

Judging by appearances, a clear, tough diamond has nothing in common with the black, flaky graphite used in pencil lead. But in actuality, these materials have everything in common. They are both made up exclusively from carbon atoms.

Carbon appears in many different forms, referred to as allotropes. In each form, atoms are arranged in different patterns within the material. They may be crystalline, with the atoms arranged in a well-organized manner; or they may be amorphous, where they have no real structure at all. Diamonds and graphite are crystalline forms of carbon. Amorphous forms of carbon include charcoal and carbon black.

To understand how carbon makes up so many different materials, it is important to look at the carbon atom. Like all elements, a carbon atom is made up of protons, neutrons, and electrons. Carbon has six of each of these. The protons and neutrons reside in the atom's nucleus, and the electrons orbit the nucleus. For carbon, two electrons follow an inner orbital path; four more electrons, known as valence electrons, follow an outer orbital path. Atoms are most stable when their

Diamonds achieve their hardness because of the way the carbon atoms are arranged.

valence layer is filled with eight electrons. Atoms can share these valence electrons with other atoms when they link together in a bond called a covalent bond.

In graphite, three of carbon's valence electrons form bonds with adjacent carbon atoms, forming sheets. The fourth electron wanders over the sheets. Since electricity is the flow of electrons, graphite's wandering electrons make it a good conductor of electricity. The graphite sheets are held together by molecular forces called van der Waals forces. These forces are weak, so the graphite sheets break apart easily, making graphite seem flaky.

The carbon atoms in a diamond arrange themselves so they share valence electrons with an atom on each corner of a tetrahedron, an arrangement that looks like a three-sided pyramid. Because all of the atoms in a diamond share these same strong bonds, diamonds are strong in all directions. Since they have no wandering electrons, diamonds do not conduct electricity well, making them good insulators.

Bucky Takes the Prize

In 1985, three professors accidentally discovered another form of carbon using a laser and a piece of graphite. They were Robert Curl and Richard Smalley

◢ Carbon Curiosities

» Carbon is the fourth most abundant element in the universe, behind hydrogen, helium, and oxygen.

» Carbon makes up 18.5 percent of the human body, but only 0.03 percent of Earth.[1]

» The pigment used in the oldest known tattoo was made from carbon.

» Of all known natural substances, diamonds are the hardest. Diamonds rate a ten on the Mohs Hardness Scale, which ranges from one (softest) to ten (hardest). Graphite is one of the softest materials, rating a one to two on the Mohs Hardness Scale.

» Car tires contain 30 percent carbon black.[2] The carbon black adds strength to the tires and helps shield the rubber molecules from UV rays.

of Rice University and Harold Kroto of the University of Sussex. The team was attempting to catalog microwave signals of materials in the lab so they could identify those same materials in space. The process used a laser to blast clusters of atoms off a solid material, which they then measured. The result of this experiment on graphite indicated there were stable molecules made of 60 and 70 carbon atoms; the 60-atom molecule, or C_{60}, was the most common. The team made a paper model of a spherical shape made from 20 hexagons and 12 pentagons. Not knowing what mathematical shape it was, they consulted the head of the math department. He replied, "What you've got there, boys, is a soccer ball."[3]

The group named the C_{60} molecule *buckminsterfullerene* because the shape looked like the geodesic domes designed by architect R. Buckminster Fuller. Before long, the new molecules earned the nickname buckyballs. While C_{60} looked like a soccer ball, C_{70} looked a bit like a rugby ball. The team also found other forms of this molecule, naming the entire class *fullerenes*.

Packed together, buckyballs create a solid with interesting properties. The solid starts out soft like graphite, but it becomes as hard as a diamond when compressed by 30 percent. The solid springs back

◂ Bucky in Space

Because buckminsterfullerene was discovered during experiments designed to catalog signals of materials in space, researchers assumed the material could be found there. However, it took 25 years for that to happen. In 2010, astronomers using NASA's Spitzer Space Telescope finally detected buckyballs in space. This original sighting found buckyballs in gas form in a planetary nebula, the remains of material that was shed by an aging star.

Two years later, astronomers using the same telescope detected the first instance of buckyballs in solid form near a pair of stars that are 6,500 light years from Earth. Astronomer Nye Evans described the find: "These buckyballs are stacked together to form a solid, like oranges in a crate."[4]

The find suggested buckyballs are more widespread than initially thought. NASA's Mike Werner said, "They may be . . . an essential building block for life, throughout the cosmos."[5]

to its original volume when the pressure is released. By itself, C_{60} is a semiconductor, but it can combine to form compounds that are insulators, semiconductors, conductors, and superconductors.

Standard solar panels are made of silicon. Thanks to buckyballs, future solar panels may be made of carbon.

Scientists are still investigating practical ways to use buckyballs. Since they are hollow and do not appear harmful to humans, they are being studied for use in targeted delivery of medications. Buckyballs are also being studied for use in clean energy such as hydrogen fuel cells and solar cells.

The discovery of this new form of carbon earned the team the 1996 Nobel Prize in Chemistry and opened the door for more carbon discoveries at the nano level.

Totally Tubular

In the early 1990s, researchers started looking at a new form of carbon nanomaterial. Richard Smalley called these particles buckytubes. They share a similar form to buckyballs, each looking like a piece of chicken wire rolled up in a tube. These structures are now commonly known as carbon nanotubes (CNTs). While CNTs usually have diameters between one and 50 nanometers, they can vary widely in length.[6]

There are many different forms of CNTs, although they generally fall into one of two categories. A single-walled carbon nanotube (SWCNT) has the same shape as a drinking straw. A multi-walled carbon nanotube (MWCNT) has multiple layers of nested nanotubes. A MWCNT can be as simple as one CNT within another, or it can have more than 100 different layers.[7]

CNTs are stronger and more flexible than steel. They conduct heat and electricity better than copper. And they do not degrade from thermal expansion and contraction, corrosion, or exposure to radiation. CNTs have already found their way into many commercial applications. They are added to sports equipment such as tennis rackets and bicycle frames to provide greater strength at a lighter weight. They are used as filters in water purifiers and to boost the performance of batteries. CNTs are also being investigated for many uses within the electronics industry. In the future, people may be able to print out their own electronics using CNT ink and their computer's printer. And CNTs may replace silicon in future computers.

A material called carbon aerogel, made of carbon nanotubes, is so light a flower can hold it up.

The Wonder Material

In the autumn of 2002 at the University of Manchester, researchers discovered yet another form of carbon. Professor Andre Geim, thinking of carbon nanotubes, metallic electronics, and graphite's electronic properties, tasked PhD student Da Jiang to "make films of graphite as thin as possible."[8] Da eventually returned with a little speck of graphite approximately ten microns thick. Dr. Geim told him it was too thick and suggested he try again. Da admitted that was all that remained of the original graphite, as he had used up the materials he had. While Dr. Geim teased Da about "polishing a mountain to get one grain of sand," a nearby student pulled some transparent tape out of the trash.[9] Under a microscope, they looked at the graphite flakes stuck to the tape and discovered some very thin layers of graphite on it.

PhD student Kostya Novoselov joined Dr. Geim in studying this new material. The pair demonstrated it was possible to obtain a layer of graphite that was one atom thick. This two-dimensional material, known as graphene, looked like a flat piece of chicken wire. The researchers' finding disproved the commonly held belief that such a substance could not be obtained at room

temperature. Their experiments also determined that graphene had a pronounced field effect, or the ability to control the conductivity of a material by applying an electric field. This is the property that made silicon the choice for computer chips.

Crank It Up

The next generation of audio speakers may be clear and flexible thanks to graphene. Unlike traditional speakers that produce sounds by inducing vibrations in a material such as metal or plastic, graphene speakers use heat. Applying alternating current to the graphene causes it to periodically heat up. This, in turn, creates temperature waves in the surrounding air, producing sound. Scientists have known about this thermoacoustic effect for a long time, but until recently there has not been a material that could make good use of it. Other speakers under development utilize this same effect using carbon nanotubes.

Graphene is the thinnest known material, yet it is 150 times stronger than steel at the same weight. It is also flexible, able to stretch to 120 percent of its length. Graphene can carry 1,000 times more electricity than copper at speeds up to 250 times that of silicon.[10] This remarkable find earned Geim and Novoselov the 2010 Nobel Prize in Physics.

Graphene's incredible properties have spurred researchers around the world to investigate ways in which graphene can be used. Potential applications include gas sensors, flexible electronics, and improved batteries and solar cells.

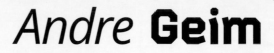

Andre **Geim**

(1958–)

A ndre Geim was born and raised in the Soviet Union. However, the Soviet government labeled him as German because he descended from German colonists. He got excellent grades in high school but was twice denied entry into one of Russia's top universities due to his German ethnicity. A short while later, he applied and was surprisingly accepted to Russia's top school for physics. The work was grueling, and the facilities were often lacking equipment and materials.

After earning his PhD, Geim worked at several universities before becoming a professor at the University of Nijmegen in the Netherlands. While at Nijmegen, he started what he called "Friday night experiments," time spent looking into ideas not related to his main research. One of these experiments, known as the levitating frog, illustrated that just about anything can be levitated using magnets if the magnet is powerful enough. It also showed that living things could be magnetically levitated without harmful effects. Geim has received many awards, including the Nobel Prize for Physics in 2010 for his discovery of graphene.

CARBON'S STRUCTURES

CARBON ATOM

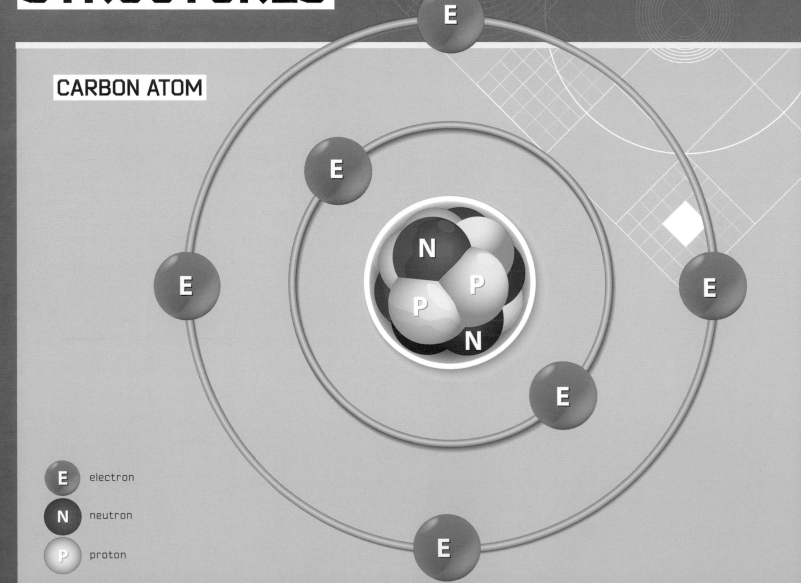

E — electron

N — neutron

P — proton

DIAMOND

BUCKMINSTERFULLERENE

GRAPHITE

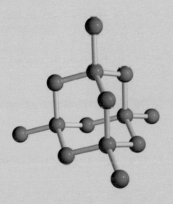

GRAPHENE

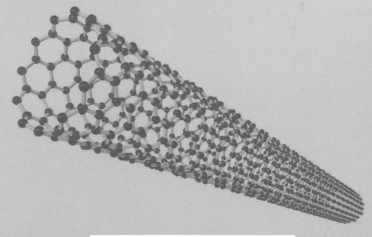

 carbon atom

CARBON NANOTUBE

FIVE

HOW SMALL CAN
COMPUTERS GO?

How many computers fit inside a thimble? If the computer in question is a Michigan Micro Mote, or M3, the answer is nearly 150. In 2015, M3 claimed the title as the smallest computer in the world, measuring two by four by four millimeters.[1] The M3 joins a new class of computers called motes or smart dust. Motes are computer sensors that detect a variable such as temperature, light, or vibrations.

There are three M3 versions. One takes pictures, records video, or detects motion. The second senses temperature, and the third senses pressure. The motes communicate wirelessly with each other and a computer base station by sending and receiving radio waves. Working together, the sensors can monitor a room for motion or temperature anomalies, transmitting that information to the base station. Although the sensors currently need to be within six feet (2 m) to communicate, the team is working on increasing their range to 65 feet (20 m).[2]

Dozens of Michigan Micro Mote computers can fit on a penny.

The M3 is a complete computer. It is able to receive input, process the input data, and, after making decisions based on the data, provide output. As Professor David Blaauw explained, "The sensors are the input and the radios are the output. The other key to being a complete computer is the ability to supply its own power."[3]

Kris Pister shows two smart dust sensors.

The M3 has a solar cell that needs only indoor light to power the battery. The team expects the M3 could run perpetually. The solar cell provides 20 nanowatts of power while the M3 uses only two nanoamps of electric current when on standby—a million times less than the average cell phone uses on standby.

The M3 is designed as layers, similar to a sandwich. By mixing and matching the layers or adding new functional layers, the team can create new motes with different functionalities at relatively low cost.

Smart Dust

The term *smart dust* was first coined in 1996 by Kris Pister of the University of California, Berkeley. He imagined programming "the walls and the furniture, and some day even the insects and the dust."[4]

The Defense Advanced Research Projects Agency (DARPA), an agency of the US Department of Defense, saw great potential in smart dust. DARPA officials imagined being able to spread these sensors throughout a battlefield, providing real-time information to soldiers in the field. Pister envisioned other uses for smart dust, including tracking living things as small as insects, detecting environmental conditions that affect crops and livestock, and managing inventory.

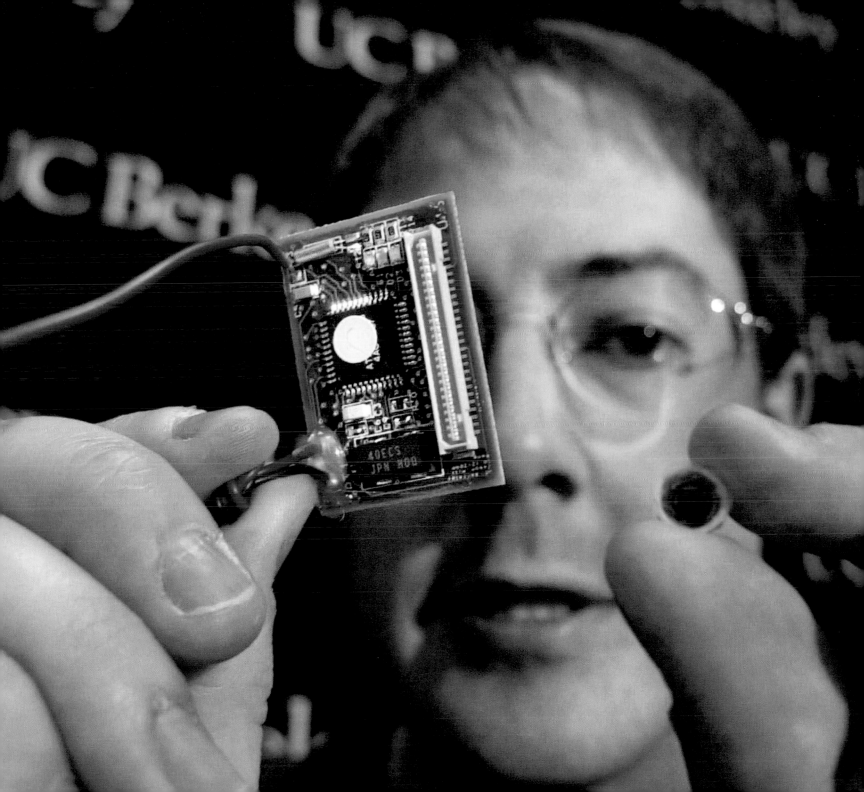

The Babbage Engine

The first computer was designed long before any computer was successfully built. In the mid-1800s, Englishman Charles Babbage started designing his Analytical Engine, a device that had many of the characteristics of modern-day computers. Babbage also designed several other automatic calculating machines. His Difference Engine No. 2 was not completed until more than 150 years after it was designed. This mechanical engine includes a calculator and a printer that documents its calculations. The device, which contains 8,000 parts, is 11 feet (3.4 m) long and weighs five short tons (4.5 metric tons).[9] There are two Babbage Engines in existence. One resides in London's Science Museum. California's Computer History Museum is home to the other.

The Michigan Micro Mote team included medical monitoring as a potential application. The precursor to the M3, the Phoenix, was designed to be inserted into the human eye to monitor pressure in people suffering from glaucoma. Dr. Blaauw imagines someday being able to view the inside of a cell. Even if computers never make their way into a cell, they have come a long way from where they began.

From Beast to Transistor

February 1946 brought the first public appearance of a general-purpose computer. People were amazed by this all-electronic calculating machine. In 30 seconds, the Electronic Numerical Integrator and Computer (ENIAC) performed calculations that previously took 12 hours with the use of a calculator.[5] It was also a beast. When operational, ENIAC weighed 30 short tons (27 metric tons) and took up more space than the average new home at the time.[6] It needed 150 kilowatts of electricity to run, prompting it to have its own dedicated power lines.[7] Today, the power ENIAC used could light more than 10,000 light bulbs.[8]

The dot on the scientist's pad is a microprocessor; 20 of these microprocessors have the same power as the ENIAC in the background.

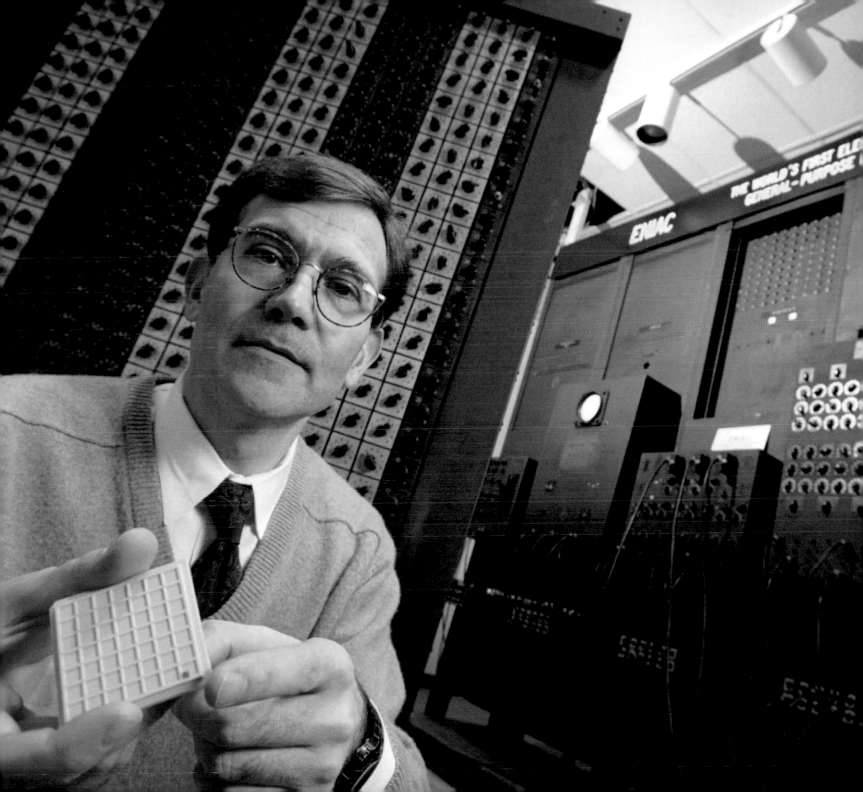

While the ENIAC performed 5,000 operations every second, it had no stored program memory.[10] Programming the ENIAC meant setting switches and changing wires around, a process that took days. It was also not particularly reliable. One of its 18,000 vacuum tubes required replacing every six hours on average.[11]

Vacuum tubes were the heart of early computers. While they looked like large light bulbs, they were actually three-terminal devices, where electric signals applied to one of the terminals controlled the electricity flowing through the other two. Computers were designed around these devices. All instructions and data were represented by either a one (the flow of electricity) or a zero (no electricity). As computers got more complicated, vacuum tubes became problematic. They were large and unreliable, and they used huge amounts of power.

In 1947, John Bardeen and Walter Brattain, researchers at Bell Telephone Laboratories, looked to semiconductors to produce smaller, more reliable, and more efficient three-terminal devices. Semiconductors conduct electricity, but not as well as conductors do. So scientists can control the flow of electricity through semiconductors better than they can through conductors. Bardeen and Brattain discovered they could create a three-terminal device called a transistor using semiconducting material. They placed two terminals very close together on the semiconducting material. A third terminal allowed the team to apply a voltage to the semiconducting material, allowing electricity to flow between the other two terminals. When the voltage was removed, the flow of electricity stopped. Bardeen and Brattain won the 1956 Nobel Prize in Physics for their work with semiconductors and the discovery of what became known as the transistor effect.

Early transistors were separate components that needed to be attached to other components to form an electronic circuit. Electronic circuits with these separate components were manufactured by

Today's integrated circuits are small enough to be built into credit cards.

hand. If just one connection was installed incorrectly, the circuit would not work. In 1958 and 1959, Jack Kirby at Texas Instruments and Robert Noyce at Fairchild Camera separately developed ways to produce an entire electronic circuit from a single material, creating the integrated circuit (IC). The use of ICs quickly produced computers that were

ENIAC-on-a-Chip

In 1996, a group of students and faculty at the University of Pennsylvania celebrated the fiftieth anniversary of the ENIAC by translating the historic computer onto an integrated chip. A comparison shows that although the ENIAC-on-a-Chip had more total elements, it was 200 times faster while using only a miniscule fraction of the space and power the original ENIAC required.[12]

	ENIAC	ENIAC-on-a-Chip
Year built	1946	1996
Vacuum tubes	18,000	None
Transistors	None	250,000
Resistors	170,000	None
Capacitors	10,000	None
Total elements	198,000	250,000
Footprint	240 sq ft (22.3 sq m)	0.00069 sq ft (0.000064 sq m)
Clock speed	100 kHz	20 MHz (20,000 kHz)
Power	174 kW	0.5 W (0.0005 kW)

smaller, faster, and more reliable than ever before. Noyce later cofounded the technology company Intel. Kirby received the Nobel Prize in Physics in 2000 for the invention of the integrated circuit; Noyce had died in 1990.

The Making of a Circuit

Virtually every electronic device used today is made up of one or more ICs. ICs are often referred to by other names such as processors, microprocessors, and chips. They all contain millions or even billions of transistors that act as switches, allowing electricity to flow or turning it off to represent ones and zeros. As with early computers, this binary logic represents instructions and data within the processor.

Before an IC is built, it goes through an extensive design process. Engineers put together a plan for the circuit and test it using computers. They use these plans to develop masks, which are essentially tiny stencils, that are used in the construction of the IC.

An IC starts with silicon, the primary element in sand. Silicon is a semiconductor; by adding impurities to silicon, scientists can change it to be either a conductor or an insulator. Sand is melted and purified so that almost all the atoms are silicon. When cooled, the silicon hardens into a single, giant crystal called an ingot. Each silicon ingot is then sliced into thin, millimeter-thick wafers. After the wafer's surface has been polished until it is flawless, it undergoes a printing process using light called photolithography.

A light-sensitive material called a photoresist is applied to the wafer's surface. UV light passes through the mask onto the wafer, imprinting the IC's pattern on it. A chemical process removes the portions of the photoresist that were exposed to the light. Impurities are introduced into the unprotected part of the silicon in a process called doping, turning the silicon into either an insulator or a conductor. The photoresist and doping process is repeated for each of the masks created during the design to build up the components in the IC.

When the silicon has been modified to account for all the components in the IC, metal is added using another photolithography process. The metal connects all the components to complete the circuit. Many ICs are fabricated together on one silicon wafer. After the process is complete, the ICs are cut apart and tested before being delivered to electronics manufacturers.

Binary Logic

In everyday life, people deal with decimal math, also known as base 10. In base 10, each digit can be any of ten possible numbers, from zero to nine. Each place value increases by a factor of 10. The lowest place value represents the number of ones. The next place value is the number of tens, the next is the number of hundreds, and so on. For example, the number 475 means there are four 100s, seven 10s, and five 1s, or 400 + 70 + 5.

Scientists dealing with computers must be familiar with binary computing. In binary math, or base 2, each digit is either zero or one, and each place value increases by a factor of 2. The lowest place value represents the number of ones. The next place value is the number of twos, the next is the number of fours, and so on. In base 2, the number 11001 means there is one 16, one 8, zero 4s, zero 2s, and one 1, or 16 + 8 + 0 + 0 + 1. Written in base 10, this number would be 25.

Base 2 works nicely with transistors, which can act as switches. When a transistor is "on" and current is flowing, it represents a one. An "off" transistor represents a zero.

The Relentless Boss

Less than a decade after the birth of the IC, an electronics engineer made an observation about the blooming industry. In 1965, Gordon Moore published a paper called "Cramming More Components onto Integrated Circuits." Moore noted that the number of components in an IC doubled every year while the price stayed the same. He predicted this trend would continue and by 1975, the number of transistors on a chip would reach 65,000.[13]

In 1975, Moore realized his estimate was a little off, so he revised it. The number of transistors on a chip would double every two years rather than one. For more than 50 years, this prediction, known as Moore's Law, has been a driving force. Mark Bohr, a leading scientist at Intel, described Moore's Law as a "relentless boss." Bohr said, "We have to continually learn how to make transistors smaller to achieve these benefits—improved performance, lower power, and lower cost per transistor."[14]

Gordon Moore holds up a vacuum tube from the mid-1960s.

Carbon Computing

Knowing they will soon reach the limit when silicon electronics can no longer be improved, scientists are heavily researching forms of carbon as silicon's replacement. In 2013, researchers at Stanford University built a microprocessor made up of carbon nanotubes (CNTs). Their studies suggest carbon nanotube transistors less than ten nanometers in size will be faster and more energy efficient than silicon. However, their microprocessor functions like a silicon chip made in the early 1970s, running more slowly and needing five times the power of current silicon chips. Much of the CNT chip was built using equipment currently used to manufacture silicon chips; however, the initial creation of CNTs is still problematic. CNTs grow in a tangled mess, and a third of the CNTs grown are conductors rather than semiconductors and, if used, will cause the chip to fail.

Many scientists believe graphene may be the better choice to replace silicon in computer chips. In 2011, IBM researchers built the first integrated circuit based on graphene. The chip was not entirely silicon-free; graphene transistors were built on a silicon wafer. The resulting chip was a radio-frequency mixer, a device the team believed could be used to improve cell phone service. Researchers around the world continue to investigate ways to produce transistors and integrated circuits made of graphene.

So far, the industry has kept up. In 1964, a chip measuring four square millimeters held 30 transistors. In 2014, Intel was squeezing up to 5.7 billion transistors onto a single chip. Transistor density jumped from 7.5 transistors per square millimeter to more than 8 million.[15] Moore offered a comparison for this growth: "If the auto industry advanced as rapidly as the semiconductor industry, a Rolls Royce would get a half a million miles per gallon, and it would be cheaper to throw it away than to park it."[16]

Many experts agree that by the mid-2020s, something will need to change. As the transistors get smaller, the quantum tunneling effect allows electricity to leak through the material when it should not. Chip manufacturers have already added fins to their transistors to account for this leakage. When the transistors get small enough, perhaps five nanometers in size, the transistors will fail to work at all.

Researchers around the world are looking for the next computer chip incarnation. Some are hopeful graphene can replace silicon while maintaining the same basic computer architecture. Others are looking at completely new architectures such as quantum computing, where binary states, the ones and zeros that currently make up computers, are replaced by multiple-level logic. One thing seems sure: the future of computing will remain firmly fixed in nanotechnology.

SIX

ON THE SURFACE

In April 2014, carmaker Nissan released a promotional video showing a paint technician taping off one side of a shiny white car. He sprayed an "innovative treatment" on the other side. The car drove through town, over wet streets, and onto a country road. It splashed through puddles and sloshed down a track that was more mud than road. Close-up shots showed the water and mud covering the untreated side and seeming not to touch the treated side. Captions on the video included "Repels water and spray . . . and everyday dirt."[1] When the car stopped, one side of it was splattered with brown spots while the other was a pristine white.

Nissan was not the only company using nanotechnology in its products, but it said it was "the first carmaker to apply the technology . . . on automotive bodywork." Nissan envisioned this coating being the first step toward the day when "drivers . . . never have to clean their car again."[2]

One side of the car has been coated with a nanotechnology treatment, while the other side has not.

Smooth and Shiny

Mercedes-Benz started using nanotechnology clear coats in 2003, long before Nissan rolled out its self-cleaning car. Rather than self-cleaning, Mercedes focused on making its cars more scratch resistant. In its process, ceramic nanoparticles spread out within the liquid clear coat. The painted car is then baked at 284 degrees Fahrenheit (140°C). During the heating process, the ceramic nanoparticles link together, forming a dense network.

Mercedes has determined the surface resists small scratches three times better than conventional coatings. In addition, the nanocoating retains its gloss 40 percent better, so the car stays smooth and shiny longer.[4]

Like a Lotus

Self-cleaning surfaces are not new. They are prevalent throughout the plant kingdom. In the 1970s, German botanist Wilhelm Barthlott noticed some of his plant samples never needed cleaning. The cleanest of them all was the lotus.

Barthlott wondered why a plant that lived in muddy water never got dirty. He found the answer under a microscope. The surface of a lotus leaf has a combination of microsized bumps and nanosized hairs. These structures, in combination with the waxy makeup of the leaf, allow dirt and water to literally roll off it.

The concept is similar to a bed of nails. If the nails are spaced closely enough, a person can lie on them without being punctured. This is what happens to a raindrop when it falls on the nano-hairs of a lotus leaf. In fact, as little as 2 percent of the raindrop actually comes into contact with the leaf's surface.[3] Since the water cannot stick to the surface, it bounces off. Dirt and debris are sucked into water drops by the surface tension of the water. The water falls off, taking the dirt with it.

Nissan's car treatment is not the only commercial use of the lotus effect. There are house paints, roof tiles, fabric treatments, and more. They are typically made of nanoparticles contained

Tiny hairs prevent water from sticking to the surface of a lotus leaf.

Hydrophobic versus Hydrophilic

A surface that repels water is said to be hydrophobic. By contrast, water adheres strongly to a surface that is hydrophilic. A material's type is determined by the contact angle formed when a water droplet rests on its surface. The contact angle is the angle formed where the water, air, and surface meet.

In a hydrophobic surface, the contact angle is greater than 90 degrees and the water droplet maintains a spherical shape. A water droplet flattens out on a hydrophilic surface, creating a contact angle less than 90 degrees.[5] Surfaces with contact angles greater than 140 degrees are said to be superhydrophobic; the lotus leaf has a contact angle of up to 170 degrees. There are approximately 300 hydrophobic plant species. Insects such as butterflies and dragonflies have wings that are superhydrophobic.[6]

within a coating material. All of them replicate the microscopically rough surface of the lotus leaf, preventing dirt and water from sticking.

These coatings do a good job of mimicking the lotus, but they have limitations. While the surface of the lotus leaf continuously replenishes itself, man-made coatings do not. Some ceramic coatings claim to permanently bond to materials such as the surfaces of cars, but others have to be replenished every year or two. Many of the coatings dry with a slight haze, making them unsuitable for glass surfaces needing high visibility. Also, the manufactured surfaces do not repel oils well. And because there is air between those nanohairs, they do not work under pressure. These limitations drove a team of Harvard researchers to look for an even better surface.

A Very Slippery Surface

Inspiration for Professor Joanna Aizenberg and her team at Harvard University's Wyss Institute came from the carnivorous pitcher plant. Unsuspecting insects climb up and around on the plant only to slide down its slippery surface and into a bowl of digestive juices. The key to the pitcher plant's success is a thin liquid film held in place by the underlying plant material.

Biomimicry Failure

Biomimicry is the concept of taking things that work well in nature and applying them to things people use. Sometimes, however, what works well for an animal does not work so well for humans. That was the case for the texture on Speedo's Fastskin II swimsuits. Speedo intended to boost a swimmer's speed by mimicking one of the ocean's fastest swimmers: the shark.

Harvard professor George Lauder performed a series of experiments on both the swimsuits and actual sharkskin. Sharkskin feels a bit like sandpaper due to the denticles, or tiny tooth-shaped ridges, that cover it. While these denticles enable sharks to swim 12 percent faster than they could without them, the rough surface of the Fastskin II slowed humans down.[8]

Although the Fastskin II suits were faster inside out, the suit's design had other benefits. When a swimmer squeezed into the suit, it streamlined his or her body. As Lauder noted, "They're so tight they could actually change your circulation and increase the venous return to the body, and they are tailored to make it easier to maintain proper posture even when tired. I'm convinced they work, but it's not because of the surface."[9]

The Wyss team developed a technology they call Slippery Liquid-Infused Porous Surfaces (SLIPS). SLIPS starts with a porous solid surface, 60 to 80 micrometers thick, made from Teflon nanofibers; Teflon is an artificial material made of carbon and fluorine. This solid looks like a bird's nest or steel wool, but the pores in the material are roughly 200 nanometers wide.[7] This surface is covered with a special liquid that fills in the pores and forms a film on top. Liquids flow over the film much as an ice skater skims over a thin layer of water resting on top of the ice. When a surface is coated in SLIPS, many materials—including water, oil, and blood—slip right off. The surface also resists bacteria, ice, and wax.

Next, the team tackled making the coating transparent. They created a honeycomb-like surface made from polystyrene, the main ingredient in Styrofoam. When covered with the same material used in SLIPS, the new surface behaves in the same manner. Because the honeycomb cells are smaller than the wavelength of visible light, the surface is invisible.

Applications for this slippery surface seem endless. It could prevent ice from building up on power lines and airplanes. Coating the inside of pipes could improve the efficiency of oil and fuel delivery. It could protect medical devices as well as optical surfaces such as solar cells, lenses, and sensors. SLIPS seems to work well even in harsh conditions such as freezing temperatures, high pressure, and UV exposure. The company SLIPS Technologies launched in June 2014 to produce the surface commercially.

Researchers demonstrate a stain-resistant shirt that uses nanotechnology to repel liquids.

In 2014, the Wyss team adapted the SLIPS technology for medical use. The new surface uses materials already approved by the Food and Drug Administration and can be applied to the smooth surfaces found on most medical devices. The process chemically attaches or tethers a layer of a dense liquid called perfluorocarbon to the surface. A second layer of liquid perfluorocarbon completes the Tethered-Liquid Perfluorocarbon surface, which they call TLP. The team tested TLP to ensure it prevented the two critical problems faced by medical devices implanted in the body: blood clotting and bacterial infection.

TLP-coated tubing implanted in pigs prevented blood from clotting for at least eight hours without the use of blood-thinning drugs. In another test, the team grew bacteria in TLP-coated tubing for more than six weeks. Fewer than one in a billion bacteria were able to stick to the surface. Out of curiosity, the team tested the surface against the gecko, one of the animal world's best climbers. The gecko could not hold on to the TLP-coated surface.

Climbing the Walls

The ability to climb walls requires surfaces with different properties than those that repel dirt and water. The feet, or other body parts, must be able to stick to the wall with strong enough adhesion to

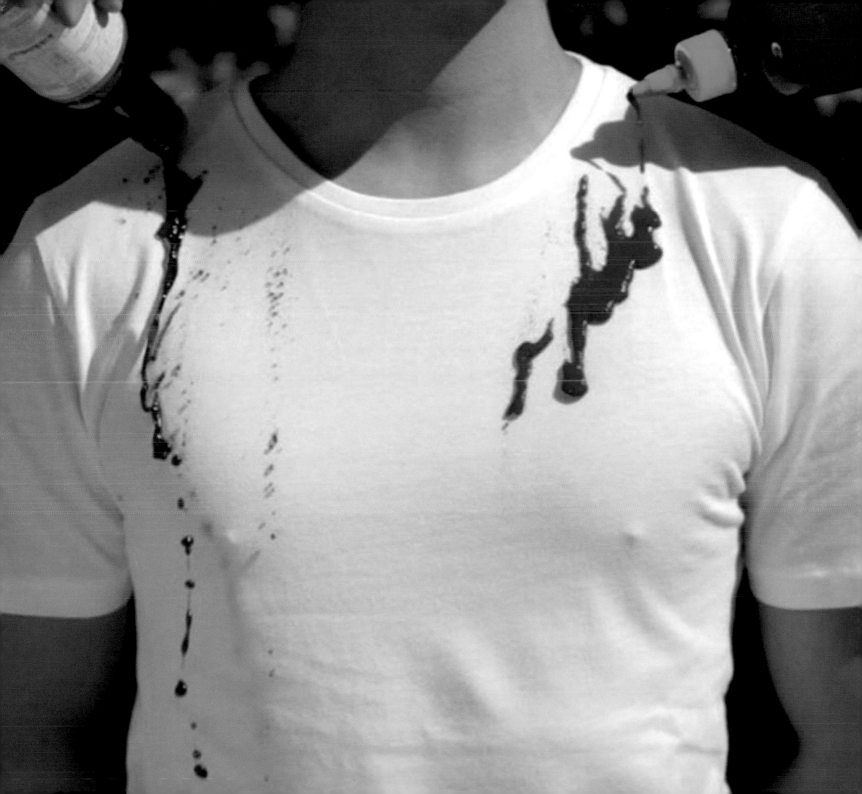

support the rest of the body. But this adhesion must also release quickly to enable the climber to move on. Many insects have this ability, as do spiders and geckos. While most insects use liquids to help them, spiders and geckos use what is called dry adhesion. Because geckos are the largest animals that have this ability, they were the perfect inspiration for humans.

In June 2014, a full-grown man accomplished the superhero feat of climbing a 25-foot- (7.6 m) tall glass wall using nothing but a set of handheld paddles.[10] The demonstration was part of DARPA's Z-Man program, a program that specifically looks to biological inspiration for ways to help soldiers scale buildings without ropes or ladders. The climbing paddles on display were inspired by gecko feet and made using nanotechnology.

Light-Sucking Surface

NASA instrument designers paint surfaces black in an attempt to prevent stray light from interfering with sensitive instruments. In 2010, NASA scientists created a surface that seemed to suck the light out of the air. Instead of flat black paint, the new surface arranges carbon nanotubes similar to yarn in a shag carpet. This structure creates tiny gaps in between the nanotubes that allow the surface to absorb 99.5 percent of the light hitting it. The result is a material that is ten times better than the paints previously used.[12] The breakthrough should allow for better scientific measurements and may allow astronomers to observe previously unseen astronomical objects.

Each toe pad on a gecko's foot is covered with curved hairs called setae. Each of these hairs is approximately 100 microns long and four microns wide. Even smaller hairs, less than 200 nanometers wide, branch off from each of these larger hairs.[11] When these hairs come into contact with a surface, they create van der Waals forces, which help the gecko stick. Van der Waals forces naturally occur between molecules. While they are normally negligible, the millions of setae on a gecko's foot create enough force to keep the gecko on a surface.

Vantablack, a product made of carbon nanotubes, absorbs 99.96 percent of light. It may help scientists take more accurate measurements.

The first scientist to successfully mimic a gecko's foot was Andre Geim. He and his University of Manchester team produced a small amount of gecko tape as one of their Friday night experiments. Using a photolithography process similar to that used to produce silicon chips, the team created a tape covered with artificial setae made of a material called kapton. One square centimeter (0.16 sq in) of tape contained approximately 100 million kapton setae and could support a one-kilogram (2.2 lb) weight.[13] The team published its findings in 2003 before shifting its focus to graphene.

SEVEN

NANOTECHNOLOGY
TO THE RESCUE

In November 2013, the press met with staff from Garrison Bespoke, a tailor shop, in a gun club in Toronto, Canada. One by one, attendees were invited to take shots at a tailored three-piece suit displayed on a mannequin. Repeated bullet hits did not penetrate the jacket.

Several days earlier, Garrison co-owner Michael Nguyen had donned the suit and allowed his employees to take turns stabbing him with a hunting knife. Nguyen remained untouched by the blade. These demonstrations proved the strength of the carbon nanotube–infused fabric used to make the suit.

Since the 1970s, Kevlar has been the material of choice for body armor. Kevlar is five times stronger than steel at the same weight.[1] Personal armor, such as a bulletproof vest, is usually made from multiple layers of Kevlar and often has an added ceramic plate for increased protection. These added layers make the armor heavy, bulky,

A man fires a gun at a bulletproof suit made with carbon nanotubes.

Thwarting Chemical Warfare

Scientists at the National Institute of Standards and Technology are developing textiles that could stave off a nerve gas attack. Nerve gases such as sarin are harmful if inhaled or absorbed through the skin. Gas trapped in clothing can later reactivate, causing problems long after the initial exposure.

The researchers showed that carbon nanotubes combined with a copper-based catalyst were capable of breaking down and thus deactivating molecules similar to those found in nerve gas. These catalytic nanotubes could be woven into clothing, breaking down the nerve gas before it reaches the person's skin.

and hot. This is not a good combination in combat situations or for those who do not want to look like they are wearing body armor.

Kevlar works by surrounding a bullet, similar to how a catcher's mitt absorbs a baseball. While the bullet stops at the Kevlar, the energy from the bullet continues on, concentrating on a relatively small area—and potentially causing blunt force trauma. This may result in bruises, cracked ribs, or other internal damage. The ceramic plate in many bulletproof vests spreads the bullet's energy out over a larger area, thereby reducing the chance of blunt force trauma.

As Dr. Liangchi Zhang, a professor at the University of Sydney in Australia, explained, "The best material for body armor should have a high level of elastic storage energy that will cause the bullet to bounce off or be deflected."[2] Dr. Zhang's experiments in 2007 indicated carbon nanotubes have this elasticity. He estimated six layers of fabric woven with carbon nanotube yarn could stop a bullet shot from a revolver. These studies indicated effective body armor could come in a fabric that looks and feels like a thin T-shirt.

The Garrison suit also uses material made of carbon nanotubes. The material is so strong the tailors had to cut the material with a band saw rather than scissors. Compared with steel at the same weight, the carbon nanotube material is 30 times stronger. But it is also approximately 50 percent lighter than Kevlar.[3]

Carbon nanotube clothing may be light and safe, but most people cannot afford to wear it. The Garrison suit costs approximately $20,000. A polo shirt from another bulletproof apparel maker costs $800.[4] One of the reasons for the high price tag is the difficulty in producing carbon nanotube–infused textiles.

Spinning Yarns

A carbon nanotube thread with a thickness one-quarter that of a human hair has tens of millions of nanotubes jammed side by side across it. Ideally, they would be aligned like pencils packed in a box. Unfortunately, carbon nanotubes are difficult to control. When produced in bulk, they develop into several dozen different types with varying material and electric properties. In addition, the nanotubes tend to form tangled clumps, which degrades their electronic properties.

Many research organizations have attempted to make carbon nanotube fibers using varying methods. In 2013, a Rice University team perfected a wet spinning process that produced a high-quality thread that holds weight and also carries electric current. Rice graduate student Dmitri Tsentalovich demonstrated the production process. The carbon nanotubes are dissolved in chlorosulfonic acid to

◂ Foaming at the Vest

Engineers at the University of California, San Diego, reported a different approach to body armor in 2013 in the form of nanofoams. These foams are not stiff like Styrofoam. Professor Yu Qiao commented, "They will appear to be less rigid but will actually be more resistant than ordinary foams."[5]

Taking a microscopic look at the nanofoams, they seem more like sponges or honeycombs. The material is riddled with holes. These pores range in size from ten nanometers to ten microns and make up between 50 and 80 percent of the structure.[6] Material made with the smaller pore sizes absorbs impact energy over the widest area, making it promising for both body armor and buildings.

A light bulb is suspended by a carbon thread that carries electric current.

form a solution with the consistency of mayonnaise. This solution is then squirted through 19 tiny holes and wound on a drum to form a string that looks like black cotton thread.[7] These threads can be made into thicker yarns to hold heavier loads or carry more electric current.

Professor Matteo Pasquali described the result of their process: "It looks like black cotton thread but behaves like both metal wires and strong carbon fibers."[8] They demonstrated this by hanging a 46-gram (1.6 oz) LED light from two carbon nanotube threads 24 micrometers thick.[9] Not only did the threads support the weight of the light; they also carried the electric current that powered the bulb.

In 2014, the Rice team reported their carbon nanotube thread carried four times more current than the same weight in copper. This could have a huge impact in aerospace applications such as airplanes and space vehicles. The cables currently used are heavy; aluminum and copper wires require steel-core reinforcement to keep them from breaking. Lighter-weight cables would produce lighter vehicles that would use less fuel.

Save That Noggin

Although carbon nanotube thread has great potential in a wide variety of applications, it cannot fully protect one of the most important parts of the body: the head. Talk of concussions usually brings to mind the National Football League, but these traumatic head injuries are also common among soldiers and hockey players. Dale Earnhardt Jr. showed even race car drivers are susceptible when he sat out several NASCAR races in 2012 to recover from a concussion. Researchers are busy looking for ways to prevent and diagnose concussions, and many are turning to nanotechnology to do so.

▴ Nanotechnology in Fashion

Not all uses of nanotechnology are practical—in some cases, they are meant to be fashionable. Researchers at EMPA, the Swiss Federal Laboratories for Materials, developed a method to coat thread with a nanometer-thin layer of gold using a plasma coating machine. Inside the machine, argon ions bombard a piece of gold, splitting off individual gold atoms. The atoms land on the polyester fiber as it is slowly pulled through the machine, coating it with a layer of gold. The resultant thread can be rolled, kinked, woven, and washed without removing the golden layer. The fabric made from the threads is soft to the touch. It is expensive, too. A necktie made from the thread, containing eight grams (0.3 oz) of gold, would sell for more than $8,000.[10]

In 2010, University of Pennsylvania researchers developed a sensor similar to a radiation badge that could be attached to a soldier's helmet to indicate exposure to an explosion that contained enough force to cause a concussion. The blast sensor relied on properties most often seen on a butterfly wing. Butterflies do not get their color from any kind of dye or pigment; the color comes from the structure of the wings and the way light reflects off them. The Pennsylvania team developed nanocrystals whose structure collapsed when exposed to frequencies associated with the supersonic blasts that accompany an explosion. Intact nanocrystals appear green; when damaged, they could appear as another color or none at all. The sensor cannot detect a concussion, but it can identify a soldier who should undergo further testing.

A PhD student at Brigham Young University took a different nanotechnological approach. In 2013, Jake Merrell developed a helmet foam containing nanoparticles. The foam not only protects the head from hard hits; it also measures the forces exerted on it. The foam, called XOnano smart foam, is piezoelectric, meaning the foam produces an electric voltage when pressure is applied to it. This information is transmitted to a tablet or computer, indicating the impact. As Merrell explained, "A coach will know within seconds exactly how hard their player just got hit. Even if a player pops up and acts fine, the folks on the sidelines will have data showing that maybe he isn't OK."[11]

Researchers at the University of Arkansas are taking concussion monitoring a step further. They developed a skullcap monitor made from carbon nanotube textiles. A football player wears the skullcap under his helmet. Coaches monitor real-time information on a computer or smartphone thanks to a wireless communication system. A pressure sensor detects impact, providing information on its location, direction, and force. Other sensors monitor pulse and blood oxygen level. Electric sensors

◢ Smart Clothing

Conductive fibers have another widespread use in the making of smart clothing. Smart clothing uses electric signals to monitor a person's body functions such as pulse, breathing rate, and stress level. This technology allows doctors to monitor the status of patients, and it helps athletes train more effectively. It could also enable the military to track the health of its soldiers, including detecting blood loss.

In the future, military helmets may contain tiny sensors that monitor soldiers' health.

track brain activity, looking for indications of dizziness, sensitivity to light, anxiety, and other neurological signs of trauma.

EIGHT

LIGHT IT UP

Nanophotonics and plasmonics are two fields of nanotechnology that study light. The quantum principle of wave-particle duality says that light acts not only like a wave but also like a particle. These light particles are called photons. Nanophotonics studies how photons and matter interact on the nanoscale. Plasmonics is a subfield of nanophotonics that studies how light can be controlled at the nanoscale using surface plasmons.

Free electrons float on the surface of metals. These electrons create a sort of ocean, complete with rippling waves called surface plasmons. Surface plasmons have a resonant frequency; if light hits them at this frequency, it makes the sea of electrons vibrate.

Macro-scale metal appears to be a specific color: gold is golden yellow, silver is a sparkly gray. Metal nanoparticles, on the other hand, appear to change color based on their size. This is due to the change in resonant frequency of their surface plasmons, one of the properties made tunable in nanoparticles due to quantum effects. When gold nanoparticles are small, the surface plasmon resonance causes them to absorb blue-green light and reflect red, making the particles appear red. As the particle size

Surface plasmons could enable future cameras to take more vivid pictures.

increases, more of the red light is absorbed, making the particles appear blue. Depending on the size of gold nanoparticles in solution, they can appear to be just about any color in the visible spectrum.

Cooking Cancer

In the 1990s, Rice University professor Naomi Halas invented a new type of gold nanoparticle. She took a glass nanosphere and encased it in gold. At the resonant frequency, the surface plasmons vibrated, causing the nanoshells to heat up. Dr. Halas could change or tune the resonant frequency of the gold nanoshells by changing the thickness of the gold coating. Then, working with bioengineering professor Jennifer West, she turned this phenomenon into a noninvasive, nontoxic way of fighting cancer.

A patient is injected with thousands of gold nanoshells. The nanoshells move through the bloodstream, seeking out the cancerous tumors and sticking to them. Within a day, all nanoshells that have not found a tumor have left the body, but the tumors are covered with them. A laser completes the treatment. It passes through human tissue without harming it. But when the light from the laser hits the nanoshells, they heat up, destroying the cancer cells.

The Rice team uses raw chicken to demonstrate how this process works. They inject a solution containing gold nanoshells into a raw chicken breast and place it under a light. A stream of steam wafts up from the injection spot where the nanoshells are heating up, cooking the chicken.

Getting Steamy

In 2013, Rice University graduate student Oara Neumann modified the gold nanoshells invented by Dr. Halas. Neumann's version "converts a broad spectrum of sunlight—both visible and invisible bandwidths—directly into heat."[1] When the nanoshells are placed in water and exposed to sunlight,

Naomi **Halas**

Growing up, Naomi Halas did not dream of being a scientist. In fact, she first majored in music when she went to college. One day, Naomi wondered where sound came from. She was told that to understand acoustics, she needed to know calculus. Halas later said, "I hadn't taken calculus. I had actually bought into this myth that . . . I probably wasn't going to be very good at math."[2]

Halas was, in fact, very good at math, and she discovered a love of science. At age 20, she switched majors. In 1980, she earned a bachelor of arts degree in chemistry from La Salle College. She went on to earn a master of arts and a PhD in physics from Bryn Mawr College.

Halas became a professor in electrical and computer engineering, biomedical engineering, chemistry, and physics and astronomy. She is the founding director for the Laboratory for Nanophotonics and a recognized world leader in plasmonics. Halas was elected to the American Academy of Arts and Sciences in 2009, the National Academy of Sciences in 2013, and the National Academy of Engineering in 2014.

they heat so quickly the water vaporizes into steam. This technology is called solar steam.

This television uses quantum dots to produce more realistic colors.

Solar steam has an energy efficiency of 24 percent. This is even better than solar cells, which typically have efficiencies around 15 percent. Solar steam converts approximately 80 percent of the sun's energy into heat, a process that enables it to produce steam from ice water.[3] The team hopes the heat can be used to sterilize medical instruments and sanitize human waste in remote areas where water treatment facilities are not available.

Halas stated, "Sanitation technology isn't glamorous, but it's a matter of life and death for 2.5 billion people." Solar steam promises to provide a technology that is "completely off-grid, that's not that large, that functions relatively quickly, is easy to handle and doesn't have dangerous components."[4]

Quantum Light

Another nanoparticle with a special relationship to light is the quantum dot (QD). QDs are nanoparticles made from a semiconducting material such as silicon. When light hits a QD, the dot converts that energy into the emission of light at a specific color determined by the QD's size. The larger the dot, the redder the light it emits; smaller dots emit bluer light.

Many applications are being developed to take advantage of the pure light emitted by QDs. When added to liquid crystal displays (LCDs), QDs provide for more vivid color over a wider spectrum. LCDs are commonly found in tablets, laptop computers, and TVs. A conventional LCD display is backlit by LEDs that emit a white light. The light passes through red, blue, green, and sometimes yellow filters to mix the color determined by a particular pixel. QD displays work the same way, but they

Holography

Holography is a type of photography that records the way an object interacts with light, displaying it later as a three-dimensional image. Most people think of scenes from movies such as *Star Wars* or *Iron Man*, but the reality of holograms is much less impressive. The colored stickers found on credit cards and paper currency are security holograms. There are also projected holograms that are created by lasers, but they are often imaged using only one color.

In 2014, researchers at the University of Cambridge in the United Kingdom used the surface plasmon resonance of silver nanoparticles to produce the first multicolored hologram projected from a surface. The team used different shapes and sizes of silver nanoparticles to control the color of light. Yunuen Montelongo indicated the development was inspired by the Lycurgus Cup, which "changes . . . color according to the position of the light source. If illuminated from one side it looks green, but if it is illuminated from the other it becomes red."[6]

start with blue light. That blue light drives the blue colors of the display; QDs provide the red and green colors.

John Volkman, marketing director for QD Vision, a company that produces QDs for displays, explained how the light works. Blue is the highest energy portion of the spectrum, "greater than red or green. You start with high energy light." The lower-energy QDs absorb the blue light, but emit only their color. Starting with lower-energy red or green to get blue would be like "pushing a rock uphill," he said.[5]

Scientists expect QDs to have a huge impact in the area of biosensing, the process that observes a person's biological functions. As with other nanoparticles, QDs can bind to antibodies to seek out specific cells when injected into a body. Each different colored dot could be associated with a different antibody, each indicating a different disease or cancer. This would allow doctors to diagnose multiple

Many currencies, such as the euro, use holograms to help prevent counterfeiting.

diseases with a single test rather than performing multiple tests—thereby saving time, money, and stress on the patient.

NINE

THE NANOFUTURE

In 2000, President Bill Clinton created the National Nanotechnology Initiative (NNI), an organization designed to coordinate nanotechnology research and development efforts among US agencies. The NNI envisions "a future in which the ability to understand and control matter at the nanoscale leads to a revolution in technology and industry that benefits society."[1] Indeed, most nanotechnology researchers imagine their work being used to make people's lives better in the future.

Nanotechnology promises to help keep people healthier on many levels. The development of stronger textiles can help protect people from traumatic injuries. Wearable sensors can notify people of the presence of dangerous particles in the air. This could include a warning to an asthma sufferer of poor air quality that could trigger an attack; it could also warn users of the presence of toxic chemicals.

Filters made of nanomaterials could clean the air and the water, removing dangerous particles before they make anyone sick. Antibacterial food packaging could keep food fresh longer. Sensors could warn people when bacteria such as *E. coli* are present in food before they eat it and get sick.

An engineer in Tanzania used nanotechnology to develop a water filtering system.

Protecting Nanoworkers

While workers strive to produce high-quality nanomaterials, governments and companies struggle to protect these workers. The Occupational Safety and Health Administration (OSHA) applies standard requirements that protect workers from potential hazards. This includes providing appropriate eye and face protection, respiratory protection, and hand protection while they handle nanomaterials.

Most of the information regarding potential hazards to workers comes from studies performed on animals. These studies indicate that carbon nanotubes and carbon black and titanium dioxide nanoparticles have the potential to contribute to possibly fatal lung problems if inhaled. Agencies tasked with protecting workers continue to study the effects of exposure to nanomaterials during manufacturing as well as safe methods for handling them.

Wild Ideas

In his famous speech in 1959, Richard Feynman mentioned "a very wild idea" one of his friends had: "[I]t would be interesting in surgery if you could swallow the surgeon."[2] Nanotechnology promises to provide such a capability.

Before diseases can be battled, they need to be detected. Scientists are working toward a "laboratory on a chip," providing the power of a hospital laboratory on a chip that people can use at home.[3] These testing devices will be not only small but also sensitive. Rather than having to wait until cancer has grown enough to be able to see it, testing devices will be able to detect a small number of cells before they are able to do much damage.

Once a disease is detected, nanomaterials will be able to fix the problem without harming any healthy tissues. Attaching antibodies to nanoparticles will enable doctors to target specific cells within the body, allowing them to deliver medicine exactly where it is needed or seek out and destroy harmful bacteria or cancer cells.

People who work with nanomaterials typically wear protective suits and masks.

Vanishing Electronics

In 2009, Dr. John Rogers from the University of Illinois, Urbana–Champaign, started working on what he calls transient electronics. These are things such as cell phones and sensors that are made of materials that dissolve completely in water or other liquids.

Dr. Rogers builds the devices on silk, a material that decomposes naturally. Rather than looking like fabric, however, this silk looks like a thin piece of plastic. Its exact structure is determined by the desired life-span of the device. A cell phone should last several years, whereas a sensor may only need to be active for weeks, days, or even minutes. The electronic components, built at the nanoscale, are made from materials such as magnesium and silicon, which are items that are easily broken down by the human body or environment.

The three main applications of transient electronics are implanted medical devices, environmental monitoring, and consumer electronics. Temporary medical devices are implanted to perform either diagnostic or therapeutic services. After a period of time, these devices are no longer needed; rather than requiring an additional surgery to remove the devices, bodily fluids break down and eliminate them. Temporary environmental sensors could be used to monitor how chemicals are dispersing during a spill or to track animals via radio tags. Consumer electronics such as cell phones and portable electronics become obsolete every few years. Rather than having these devices potentially leaking dangerous chemicals in landfills, they could be made of materials that degrade harmlessly.

Cleaner Earth

Researchers are turning to nanotechnology to improve Earth's environment. The use of lighter materials in cars, trucks, and planes could reduce the amount of fuel consumed in travel. Nanoparticles added to batteries promise to increase their lives, reducing the amount of waste produced by our electronic society. Nanoparticles show great promise in clean energy; scientists are already anticipating a bright future with innovations such as paint-on solar cells.

Scientists are also turning to nanomaterials to clean up environmental disasters. Carbon nanotube sponges are being tested for their ability to remove contaminants such as pesticides, pharmaceuticals,

Researchers are working on tiny devices, built with nanoscale components, that can be implanted into people's bodies to monitor their health.

and oil from water. Squeezing the contaminant out of the carbon nanotube sponge allows the sponge to be reused, similar to how a kitchen sponge can be reused. Other nanomaterials are being investigated for use in cleaning up toxic waste, from oil spills to radioactive materials.

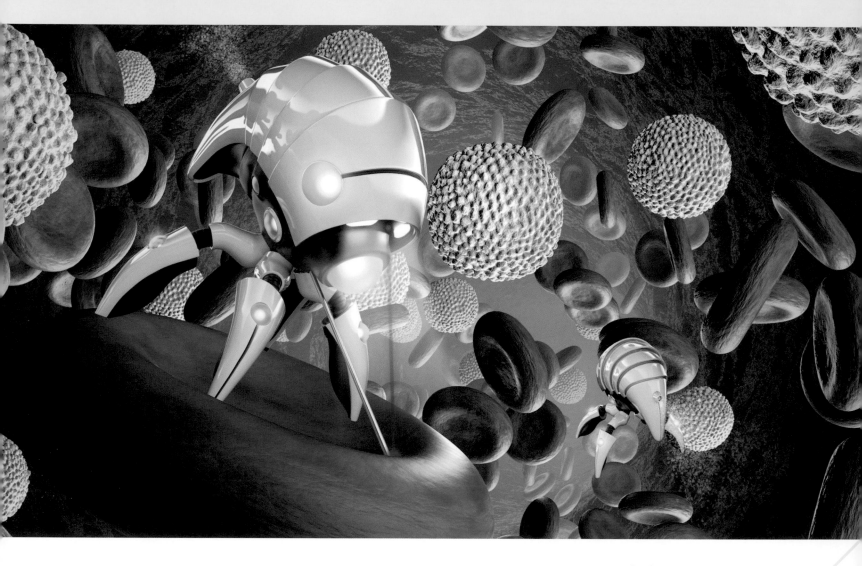

Nanoscale rust particles are being tested for their ability to remove arsenic, a poisonous material, from contaminated water. Carbon nanotubes and graphene sheets are also being tested for use in water filtration, including the desalination of seawater to forestall predicted shortages of drinking water throughout the world.

In the future, nanomaterials may be able to fight viruses and repair cells.

Shape-Shifting Nanotech

After a toy loses its appeal, it either finds its way into more appreciative hands or into a landfill. What if that toy could be changed into something new? If a team of Carnegie Mellon University (CMU) and Intel researchers is successful, this will be the future.

Continuing work started in 2002, the team is working on programmable matter called *catoms*, short for claytronic atoms. The team envisions tiny balls, or even particles the size of a grain of sand, that can reconfigure themselves and change their color to match an image. This technology would allow for shape-shifting furniture and toys. The technology, when paired with video conferencing, could also revolutionize communication. Rather than speaking with a person's image on a screen, one could interact with a catom version of that person.

Senior researcher Jason Campbell described a potential use: "Think of a mobile device. My cell phone is too big to fit comfortably in my pocket and too small for my fingers. It's worse if I try to watch movies or do my e-mail. But if I had 200 to 300 milliliters of catoms, I could have it take on the shape of the device that I need at that moment."[5]

A Future Yet to Be Imagined

Prior to creating the NNI, President Clinton tasked the Interagency Working Group on Nanoscience, Engineering and Technology (IWGN) to investigate how best to coordinate nanotechnology research and development. In its report, the IWGN stated, "Nanotechnology could impact the production of virtually every human-made object—everything from automobiles, tires, and computer circuits to advanced medicines and tissue replacements—and lead to the invention of objects yet to be imagined."[4]

Researchers are already imagining remarkable products, and there are surely more to come. People will be able to change the color of a car, a computer, and even clothing with the touch of a button. Structures will be able to transmit a warning when a potential failure is detected. Containers will be able to repair cracks on their surfaces before they leak toxic materials. Real-life invisibility cloaks may hide soldiers or undesirable sights, while gecko paddles will enable people to scale buildings. Nanotechnological advances in food could allow healthful foods to taste like decadent desserts, while futuristic clothing may provide people with wearable heating and air conditioning.

If nanowires were woven into clothing, people could use less energy heating buildings.

Nanodangers

Nanotechnology pioneer Eric Drexler once stated, "Every major advance in making things can have both beneficial and harmful applications, and even beneficial applications have unintended (and often unpredictable) consequences."[6] So how can the world reap the rewards of nanotechnology while preventing harm? For his part, Drexler cofounded the Foresight Institute in 1986, a nonprofit, nongovernmental organization designed to encourage beneficial development of nanotechnology.

The Center for Responsible Nanotechnology (CRN) is another think tank dedicated to responsibly developing nanotechnology. The CRN states, "Although nanotechnology carries great promise, unwise or malicious use could seriously threaten the survival of the human race."[7] The network of scientists and interested individuals who make up CRN strive to raise awareness of the benefits and dangers of nanotechnology while providing plans and suggestions for restrictions to ensure the technology is used for good.

While the Foresight Institute and CRN promote beneficial nanotechnology, governments are struggling to keep up. The Project on Emerging Nanotechnologies (PEN), another organization dedicated to the responsible development of nanotechnology, indicated in 2008 that the Consumer Product Safety Commission was not prepared to deal with products containing nanomaterials. Harvard University's E. Marla Fletcher reported, "The agency lacks the budget, the [legal] authority, and the

Silver Lining?

In 2013, the National Resources Defense Council (NRDC) successfully challenged the Environmental Protection Agency (EPA) with regard to a company's use of nanosilver. Silver is known to be a strong antimicrobial agent, killing both bad and beneficial bacteria.

The US court system agreed with the NRDC that the EPA had allowed a textile company to use nanosilver when it should have further investigated the potential risks of the use. This is sure to be one of many instances in which the widespread use of nanotechnology will be challenged.

scientific expertise to ensure the hundreds of nanoproducts now on the market . . . are safe. This problem will only worsen as more sophisticated nanotechnology based products begin to enter the consumer market."[8]

Organizations such as Friends of the Earth and Center for Food Safety strive to slow down the release of nanotechnology into the world until it is better understood. Ready or not, nanoparticles are already being released into the environment. In addition to the thousands of consumer products containing nanomaterials, systems using nanoparticles to remove microbes and toxins from water are already being tested in countries including Mexico and India.

Some groups are concerned about the safety of products containing nanosilver.

Without a doubt, the world's future is entwined with nanotechnology. It looks to be the next technological revolution. Like scientific revolutions before it, its path will likely not be smooth—and the results will be unimaginable. A hundred years from now, people will look back and wonder how their ancestors managed to survive without the wonders of nanotechnology.

ESSENTIAL FACTS

Key Discoveries

» **Electron microscopy:** The use of electrons to "view" materials eliminates the optical limits hindering light microscopes, enabling scientists to view nanoscale objects.

» **Integrated circuit:** The integrated circuit combines all components of an electronic circuit on a single piece of semiconductor material.

» **The lotus effect:** The self-cleaning ability of the lotus leaf is due to micro- and nanosized structures on the leaf that prevent water from adhering to it.

» **Quantum mechanics:** Quantum mechanics are the laws of physics stating that matter, especially at the molecular or atomic level, displays behavior of both particles and waves.

Key Players

» **Intel Corporation:** Intel is a world leader in the design and production of semiconductor chips. Gordon Moore, the creator of Moore's Law, is one of Intel's founders.

» **Rice University:** Many of the world's leaders in nanotechnology teach and conduct research at Rice University, the location of the discovery of buckyballs. Naomi Halas is the director of the Smalley Institute for Nanoscale Science and Technology and founding director of Rice's Laboratory for Nanophotonics.

» **University of Manchester:** The University of Manchester is the academic home of Andre Geim and Kostya Novoselov, discoverers of the two-dimensional carbon material graphene. The university is also home to the National Graphene Institute, a research and incubator center dedicated to the development of graphene and its applications.

Key Tools and Technologies

» **Bottom-up nanofabrication:** Bottom-up nanofabrication is the production of nanomaterials achieved by building materials up at the atomic or molecular level. This is usually one of many complicated chemical processes that result in the desired nanomaterial.

» **Photolithography:** Photolithography is the process by which light is used to transfer patterns onto a surface. The fabrication of semiconductor electronic chips relies heavily on photolithography.

» **Scanning probe microscopes:** Scanning probe microscopes are a class of microscopes that use a probing element that allows scientists to see the molecules and atoms on the surfaces of materials.

» **Top-down nanofabrication:** Top-down nanofabrication is the production of nanomaterials by starting with macro-scale materials and breaking them down into nanosized components.

Future Outlook

Most people agree that nanotechnology will change just about everything humans make and may usher in the next industrial revolution. While scientists envision their work contributing to a better society, there are concerns that the technology could be used for harm on a spectacular scale.

Quote

"Nanotechnology could impact the production of virtually every human-made object . . . and lead to the invention of objects yet to be imagined."

—*The Interagency Working Group on Nanoscience, Engineering and Technology*

GLOSSARY

antibody

A protein produced by the body in response to a foreign antigen such as a bacterium or toxin.

atom

The smallest unit of a chemical element.

catalyst

A substance that affects the speed of a chemical reaction without being affected itself.

ceramic

A hard, brittle material formed by firing clay or similar substances.

electronic circuit

A complete path through which an electric current can flow.

element

A substance that consists of atoms of only one kind as defined in the periodic table.

insulator

A material through which electricity does not flow easily.

ion

An atom that has an electric charge; this occurs when the number of electrons is not equal to the number of protons.

latent

Present but not yet apparent or active.

lens

A device that diverges or converges beams of light or electrons.

micron

A micrometer, one millionth of a meter.

molecule

The smallest physical unit of a substance. This can be one or more atoms of an element or two or more atoms of a compound.

photon

A particle of light.

pixel

The smallest unit used to build an image on a visual display unit such as a television or computer screen.

vacuum

A space in which there is no air or gas.

ADDITIONAL RESOURCES

Selected Bibliography

"Andre Geim—Nobel Lecture: Random Walk to Graphene." *Nobelprize.org*. Nobel Media AB, 2014. Web. 12 May 2015.

Bhushan, Bharat. "NanoBiomimetics: Turning Nature's Successes into Gold." *nano*. Nanomagazine, n.d. Web. 1 Apr. 2015.

Kelley, Shana, and Ted Sargent. *An Introduction to Nanotechnology: The New Science of Small*. University of Toronto. *The Great Courses*, 2012. DVD.

"Microscopy Resource Center." *Olympus*. Olympus America, n.d. Web. 22 Apr. 2015.

Further Readings

Gibilisco, Stan. *Optics Demystified*. New York: McGraw-Hill, 2009. Print.

Orzel, Chad. *How to Teach Physics to Your Dog*. New York: Scribner, 2009. Print.

Ottaviani, Jim, Leland Myrick, and Hilary Sycamore. *Feynman*. New York: First Second, 2011. Print.

Parsons, Paul, and Gail Dixon. *The Periodic Table: A Visual Guide to the Elements*. New York: Quercus, 2014. Print.

Websites

To learn more about Cutting-Edge Science and Technology, visit **booklinks.abdopublishing.com**. These links are routinely monitored and updated to provide the most current information available

For More Information

For more information on this subject, contact or visit the following organizations:

National Nanotechnology Infrastructure Network

250 Duffield Hall
Cornell University
Ithaca, NY 14853
607-255-2329
http://www.nnin.org

The National Nanotechnology Infrastructure Network (NNIN) is a partnership of advanced nanotechnology facilities, located throughout the United States. Supported by the National Science Foundation, the NNIN is a research facilitator and coordinator of education outreach in all areas of nanoscience.

National Nanotechnology Initiative

4201 Wilson Boulevard
Stafford II Room 405
Arlington, VA 22230
703-292-8626
http://www.nano.gov

This federal program coordinates nanotechnology-related research and development activities occurring throughout government agencies.

SOURCE NOTES

Chapter 1. Tiny Technology

1. Sindy Tang. "The Rocket Swimsuit: Speedo's LZR Racer." *Science in the News*. Science in the News, 15 Sept. 2008. Web. 3 Aug. 2015.

2. Kathy Barnstorff. "Olympic Swimmers Shattering Records in NASA-Tested Suit." *Phys.org*. Science X Network, 18 Aug. 2008. Web. 3 Aug. 2015.

3. Janet Bealer Rodie. "Ultra Tech, Ultra Speed." *Textile World*. Billian Publishing, n.d. Web. 3 Aug. 2015.

4. "Sleek Swimsuits, Inspired by Penguins." *Specialty Fabrics Review*. Industrial Fabrics Association International, 1 May 2011. Web. 3 Aug. 2015.

5. "What Is Nanotechnology?" *Nano.gov*. United States National Nanotechnology Initiative, n.d. Web. 3 Aug. 2015.

6. Michael Dumas. "Viruses Come in All Shapes, Sizes, and Languages!" *University of Delaware*. University of Delaware, n.d. Web. 3 Aug. 2015.

7. K. Eric Drexler. "A Radical Future for Nanotechnology." *World Future Society*. World Future Society, n.d. Web. 3 Aug. 2015.

8. Richard Feynman. "There's Plenty of Room at the Bottom." *Wiley*. John Wiley & Sons, n.d. Web. 3 Aug. 2015.

9. Ibid.

10. "Consumer Products Inventory." *The Project on Emerging Nanotechnologies*. The Project on Emerging Nanotechnologies, n.d. Web. 3 Aug. 2015.

11. Richard Feynman. "Appendix F — Personal Observations on the Reliability of the Shuttle." *Kennedy Space Center*. National Aeronautics and Space Administration, n.d. Web. 3 Aug. 2015.

Chapter 2. Viewing the Nanoverse

1. "Scanning Tunneling Microscope." *IBM*. IBM, n.d. Web. 3 Aug. 2015.

2. "From Thrilling Toy to Important Tool." *Nobelprize.org*. Nobel Media AB, n.d. Web. 3 Aug. 2015.

3. "The Electromagnetic Spectrum." *Imagine the Universe*. National Aeronautics and Space Administration, Mar. 2013. Web. 3 Aug. 2015.

4. "What Is Resolution?" *Miami University*. Miami University, n.d. Web. 3 Aug. 2015.

5. Dave Mosher. "Tiny Spheres Turn Regular Microscopes into Nanoscopes." *Wired*. Condé Nast, 1 Mar. 2011. Web. 3 Aug. 2015.

6. Ibid.

7. "Types of Microscopy." *Center for Probing the Nanoscale*. Stanford University, n.d. Web. 3 Aug 2015.

8. "Press Release: The 1986 Nobel Prize in Physics." *Nobelprize.org*. Nobel Media AB, 2014. Web. 3 Aug. 2015.

Chapter 3. Nanoparticles

1. Steve Jurvetson. "Why You Should Care about Molecular Nanotechnology." *Foresight Institute*. Foresight Institute, n.d. Web. 3 Aug. 2015.

2. Holly Cave. "The Nanotechnology in Your Sunscreen." *The Guardian*. Guardian News and Media Limited, 13 Mar. 2014. Web. 3 Aug. 2015.

3. "Nanomaterials in Sunscreens." *EWG*. EWG, n.d. Web. 3 Aug. 2015.

4. Whitney Fitzsimmons. "Sunscreen Nanoparticles May Be Broken Down by Immune System, Research Shows." *ABC News*. Australian Broadcasting Corporation, 10 Feb. 2014. Web. 3 Aug. 2015.

Chapter 4. Carbon Craze

1. "Common Elements Important in Living Organisms." *HyperPhysics*. Georgia State University, n.d. Web. 3 Aug. 2015.

2. "What Do We Need to Make a Tire?" *Bridgestone*. Bridgestone Americas Tire Operations, n.d. Web. 3 Aug. 2015.

3. "The Discovery of Buckminsterfullerene." *Learn Chemistry*. Royal Society of Chemistry, n.d. Web. 3 Aug. 2015.

4. Trent J.Perrotto, Whitney Clavin, and Robert Massey. "NASA's Spitzer Finds Solid Buckyballs in Space." *National Aeronautics and Space Administration*. National Aeronautics and Space Administration, n.d. Web. 3 Aug. 2015.

5. Ibid.

6. "The Strongest, Lightest and Most Conductive Material Known." *Nanocomp*. Nanocomp Technologies, Inc., n.d. Web. 3 Aug. 2015.

7. "Technology Overview." *nanoScience*. Nanoscience Instruments, n.d. Web. 3 Aug. 2015.

8. "Andre Geim — Nobel Lecture: Random Walk to Graphene." *Nobelprize.org*. Nobel Media AB, 2014. Web. 3 Aug 2015.

9. Ibid.

10. John Colapinto. "Graphene: Fast, Strong, Cheap, and Impossible to Use." *The New Yorker*. Condé Nast, 22 Dec. 2014. Web. 3 Aug. 2015.

Chapter 5. How Small Can Computers Go?

1. "Michigan Micro Mote (M3) Makes History." *Electrical Engineering and Computer Science*. Regents of the University of Michigan, n.d. Web. 3 Aug. 2015.

2. Ibid.

3. Ibid.

4. Dag Spicer. "The World's Smallest Computer." *Computer History Museum*. Computer History Museum, n.d. Web. 3 Aug. 2015.

5. "ENIAC: Celebrating Penn Engineering History." *University of Pennsylvania*. University of Pennsylvania, n.d. Web. 3 Aug. 2015.

6. Evan Lerner. "ENIAC Day to Celebrate Dedication of Penn's Historic Computer." *Penn Current*. Penn Current, 10 Feb. 2011. Web. 3 Aug. 2015.

7. "ENIAC: Celebrating Penn Engineering History." *University of Pennsylvania*. University of Pennsylvania, n.d. Web. 3 Aug. 2015.

8. "LED Light Bulbs: Comparison Chart." *Eartheasy*. Eartheasy.com, n.d. Web. 3 Aug. 2015.

9. "The Babbage Engine." *Computer History Museum*. Computer History Museum, n.d. Web. 3 Aug. 2015.

10. Mike Muuss. "The History of Computing at BRL." *Army Research Laboratory*. US Army Research Laboratory, n.d. Web. 3 Aug. 2015.

11. Ibid.

12. Jan Van Der Spiegel. "ENIAC-on-a-Chip." *University of Pennsylvania*. University of Pennsylvania, Mar. 1996. Web. 3 Aug. 2015.

13. Gordon E. Moore. "Cramming More Components onto Integrated Circuits." *University of Pennsylvania*. University of Pennsylvania, n.d. Web. 3 Aug. 2015.

SOURCE NOTES CONTINUED

14. Laura Sydell. "At 50 Years Old, the Challenge to Keep Up With Moore's Law." *NPR*. NPR, 20 Apr. 2015. Web. 3 Aug. 2015.

15. Ian Cutress. "Intel Xeon E5-2687W v3 and E5-2650 v3 Review: Haswell-EP with 10 Cores." *AnandTech*. Purch, 13 Oct. 2014. Web. 3 Aug. 2015.

16. "The History of the Integrated Circuit." *Nobelprize.org*. Nobel Media AB, 2014. Web. 3 Aug. 2015.

Chapter 6. On the Surface

1. "Nissan Shows Self-Cleaning Car Coated in Nano Paint." *Autoblog*. AOL, 24 Apr. 2014. Web. 3 Aug. 2015.

2. Ibid.

3. Lisa Zyga. "Scientists Confirm Role of Nano-Hairs in Self-Cleaning Lotus Leaf." *Phys.org*. Science X Network, 17 Feb. 2006. Web. 3 Aug. 2015.

4. Jim Kerr. "Nano Paint Technology." *Chronicle Herald*. Chronicle Herald, 22 Aug. 2012. Web. 3 Aug. 2015.

5. "Contact Angle, Wetting, and Spreading." *Kino*. USA KINO Industry Co., n.d. Web. 3 Aug. 2015.

6. "Nanotechnology Solutions for Self-Cleaning, Dirt, and Water-Repellent Coatings." *Nanowerk*. Nanowerk, 11 Jan. 2011. Web. 3 Aug. 2015.

7. Tom McKeag. "Return of the Swamp Thing." *Center for Biologically Inspired Design*. Center for Biologically Inspired Design, n.d. Web. 3 Aug. 2015.

8. Sharon Begley. "Swimsuits that Turn Athletes into Barracudas." *Reuters*. Thomson Reuters, 17 July 2012. Web. 3 Aug. 2015.

9. Peter Reuell. "A Swimsuit Like Shark Skin? Not So Fast." *Harvard Gazette*. The President and Fellows of Harvard College, 9 Feb. 2012. Web. 3 Aug. 2015.

10. "DARPA Z-Man Program Demonstrates Human Climbing Like Geckos." *Defense Advanced Research Projects Agency*. US Department of Defense, 5 Jun. 2014. Web. 3 Aug. 2015.

11. Ibid.

12. Lori J. Keesey. "Blacker Than Black." *National Aeronautics and Space Administration*. National Aeronautics and Space Administration, 2 Dec. 2010. Web. 3 Aug. 2015.

13. Will Knight. "Gecko Tape Will Stick You to Ceiling." *New Scientist*. Reed Business Information, 1 Jun. 2003. Web. 3 Aug. 2015.

Chapter 7. Nanotechnology to the Rescue

1. Jeremy Pearce. "Stephanie L. Kwolek, Inventor of Kevlar, Is Dead at 90." *New York Times*. New York Times Company, 20 June 2014. Web. 3 Aug. 2015.

2. Michael Berger. "Bullets Harmlessly Bouncing off Nanotechnology T-shirts." *Nanowerk*. Nanowerk, 1 Nov. 2007. Web. 3 Aug. 2015.

3. Cameron Williamson. "Toronto Tailor Introduces Bulletproof Three-Piece Suits." *The Globe and Mail*. The Globe and Mail, 5 Nov. 2013. Web. 3 Aug. 2015.

4. Ibid.

5. Ioana Patringenaru. "Engineers Develop Nanofoams for Better Body Armor, Layers of Protection for Buildings." *UC San Diego News Center*. Regents of the University of California, 25 Mar. 2013. Web. 3 Aug. 2015.

6. Ibid.

7. "VIDEO: Carbon Nanotube Fibre Breakthrough." *Innovation in Textiles*. Innovation in Textiles, 16 Jan. 2013. Web. 3 Aug. 2015.

8. Ibid.

9. Katherine Bourzac. "Nanotubes Turned into Super Fibers." *MIT Technology Review*. MIT Technology Review, 10 Jan. 2013. Web. 3 Aug. 2015.

10. Randolph Jonsson. "Swiss Team Engineers First Weavable, Washable, Wearable Pure Gold-Coated Fiber." *Gizmag*. Gizmag, 2 Nov. 2011. Web. 3 Aug. 2015.

11. "Nanotechnology Embedded in Football Helmets Gives Real-Time Results." *Nanowerk*. Nanowerk, 6 Nov. 2013. Web. 3 Aug. 2015.

Chapter 8. Light It Up

1. James Ayre. "Solar Steam — Off-Grid Solar-Powered Sterilization System Created." *CleanTechnica*. Sustainable Enterprises Media, 24 Jul. 2013. Web. 3 Aug. 2015.

2. "Profile: Naomi Halas." *NOVA*. WGBH Educational Foundation, 19 Apr. 2005. Web. 3 Aug. 2015.

3. Ibid.

4. Ibid.

5. Tim Moynihan. "What are Quantum Dots and Why Do I Want Them in My TV?" *Wired*. Condé Nast, 19 Jan. 2015. Web. 3 Aug. 2015.

6. Lisa Zyga. "Color Hologram Uses Plasmonic Nanoparticles to Store Large Amounts of Information." *Phys.org*. Science X Network, 21 Aug. 2014. Web. 3 Aug. 2015.

Chapter 9. The Nanofuture

1. "About the NNI." *Nano.gov*. United States National Nanotechnology Initiative, n.d. Web. 3 Aug. 2015.

2. Richard Feynman. "There's Plenty of Room at the Bottom." *Wiley*. John Wiley & Sons, n.d. Web. 3 Aug. 2015.

3. Michio Kaku. *Physics of the Future: How Science Will Shape Human Destiny and Our Daily Lives by the Year 2100*. New York: Doubleday, 2011. Print. 186–187.

4. "Nanotechnology Research Directions: IWGN Workshop Report." *World Technology Evaluation Center*. World Technology Evaluation Center, Sept. 1999. Web. 6 Oct. 2015.

5. Michio Kaku. *Physics of the Future: How Science Will Shape Human Destiny and Our Daily Lives by the Year 2100*. New York: Doubleday, 2011. Print. 197.

6. Eric Drexler. "Big Nanotech: An Unexpected Future." *The Guardian*. Guardian News and Media Limited, 28 Oct. 2013. Web. 3 Aug. 2015.

7. "Index." *Center for Responsible Nanotechnology*. Center for Responsible Nanotechnology, n.d. Web. 3 Aug. 2015.

8. "Consumer Product Safety Commission Not Ready for Nanotech." *Project on Emerging Nanotechnologies*. Project on Emerging Nanotechnologies, 21 Aug. 2008. Web. 3 Aug. 2015.

INDEX

About the Author

For most of her life, Janet Slingerland did not consider herself a writer even though she was often writing. Before turning her attention to children's books, Janet was an engineer, programming microchips embedded in things such as telephones and airplanes. Janet lives in New Jersey with her husband and three children.